D1590427

CAMPAIGN TRADING

Campaign Trading
Tactics and Strategies to Exploit the Markets

John Sweeney

JOHN WILEY & SONS, INC.

New York • Chichester • Brisbane • Toronto • Singapore

This text is printed on acid-free paper.

Copyright © 1996 by John Sweeney
Published by John Wiley & Sons, Inc.

Library of Congress Cataloging-in-Publication Data:

Sweeney, John.
    Campaign trading : tactics & strategies to exploit the markets /
by John Sweeney.
      p.   cm.—(Wiley finance editions)
    Includes index.
    ISBN 0-471-14150-X (alk. paper)
    1. Program trading (Securities) 2. Investment analysis. 3. Stock
exchanges—Data processing. 4. Commodity exchanges—Data
processing. I. Title. II. Series.
HG4515.5.S93 1996
332.6'0285—dc20   96-7807

Printed in the United States of America

10 9 8 7 6 5 4 3 2 1

This book is dedicated to the folks who provided the education I didn't get in business school: Jack Hutson, Jake Bernstein, Bruce Babcock, Cliff Sherry, John Ehlers, Larry MacMillan, Martin Pring, Ned Davis, and Thom Hartle. Each provided some practical piece of the market puzzle. Thanks!

Contents

Illustrations

Introduction

Up until now, you didn't really know where to put your stops. You didn't know when to get out or to reverse. You might have had some gut feeling for it, perhaps some support or resistance levels on the chart, or perhaps a money management stop or a parabolic being crossed, or maybe you just got a signal in the other direction, but aside from reversing, these were and are vague.

What sense did it make to put your stop at the level every other trader was watching? Where did that dollar limit or percentage of capital limit on losses come from, truly? If you investigated, you found that the foundations of these practices—if you could find any—were weak. Nevertheless, the trading maxim was "Cut your losses!" How to do it?

STOPS

Here are some answers:

1. If you look at the market's price behavior from the point of entry of your trading rules, there should be some regularity.
2. One of those points of regularity is that good trades don't go very far against you. Measured properly, the difference be-

tween good trades and bad trades tells you where to put your stops.

3. Knowing where to put your stops quantifies your loss levels, which in turn gives you the amount of capital you need to trade according to the rules you're considering.

4. Knowing the losses you should be taking, you have rules against which to measure your performance. If you're managing other traders, you have standards for their performance.

MORE MARKETS, MORE TRADES

Furthermore, this technique works not just for trend trades but also for trades in all phases of the market: trades into a range, trades against the trend, and trades reversing other trades. In other words, the technique makes it possible to trade no matter what the market is doing.

Trading all the time is a new ball game. You may have several types of trades at the same time. The number of contracts or blocks of stock may vary by type of trade. The instruments themselves may vary as options or other derivatives are used. Perhaps you're trading more than one market, and each market has its own set of effective rules and loss levels. In other words, you're running a complex but necessarily coordinated trading campaign.

PREPARING TO CAMPAIGN

Running a trading campaign is not like executing a single trading rule over and over, and this book doesn't describe running a campaign. Instead, this book shows by example how to build the base for campaigning: the measurement techniques to use, how to test trading rules for effectiveness, and how to pick the types of trades you will use in future campaigns. Think of this book as an example of preparing a campaign of trading.

INNOVATION

I believe the unique argument[1] here is that we should try to capture our experience in the market with observational statistics (not parametric statistics).[2] We are still in the observational stage of developing a theory of market behavior, but that doesn't stop us from using our observations to quantify old saws like "cut your losses short," "let your profits run," and so forth. If nothing else, our computer power allows the efficient gathering of data in volumes unimaginable even a decade ago. That's experience in digital format. What we make of this experience depends on our analytical constructs. I believe I can show at least one method of analysis of our experience in the markets that gives us quantitative guides to our future conduct.

The counterargument is that markets don't behave consistently, and therefore, our experience of markets cannot be consistent. In this view, the multitude of random events stimulating the market makes its behavior unpredictable. If it's unpredictable, how is it possible to characterize it and, hopefully, exploit that characterization?

I don't argue that I can predict tomorrow's market (and I don't deny it either!), only that given my view of the market (or your view or any other consistent view—even, perhaps, a random view), it may be possible to describe the market's behavior characteristically and, for practical purposes, exploit the most likely behavior, allowing always for being wrong.

---

[1] Unique in 1982. Although there hasn't been much response to my articles in *Stocks and Commodities* magazine, good analysts started to publish work along this line in 1994 and 1995. Also, it could be argued that Art Merrill's work estimating the value of indicators at different confidence levels is in this line of thought. Ed Gotthelf's 1950s observations on how far trades carry is also experiential.

[2] *Nonparametric* statistics are used to describe phenomena that do not have normal relative frequency distributions. *Parametric* statistics are used to describe phenomena whose characteristics can be described with normal distributions (among other assumptions). These descriptions can use formulae filled with parameters, values that determine the shape of the distributions.

NINETY-NINE PERCENT PERSPIRATION

In 1982, seeking to deal with losses, I first hit on the differing behavior of winning and losing trades. I published that material in 1985 and again in 1991 and 1992. In the era of "rocket science," my down-in-the-mud techniques didn't give me much pride, but I gradually gained respect for their practicality. These days, the growth of arcane technique is unbridled, and I commend the exploration. Sooner or later, though, it all must actually work in a market where pricing is determined instant by instant by, in some cases, two people screaming at each other. This perspective reminds us that fear and greed, possessed by every investor, every trader, and every speculator, still drive the prices we seek to predict and drive them episodically, not randomly. Lots can go wrong. A certain caution, a certain humility, and a certain respect for the difficult job of exploiting changes in price is in order.

CAMPAIGN TRADING

1
Campaigning

INTRODUCTION

This is a book for speculative traders, retail or commercial, not niche traders or arbitrageurs. Speculative traders may be trading from an intensive knowledge of their market or merely from the action. Their horizon is usually short, but in some industries (copper comes to mind) may extend to four or five years. Speculative traders aim to profit from price fluctuation, not hedging. It follows that the more fluctuation they may exploit, the better their chances.

In the trading books of the early part of the century, writers would grandly refer to a campaign of trading, a series of battles and skirmishes to accumulate and eventually distribute a position, long or short. Today, while large operators still assemble and disassemble large outright positions, grand campaigning may be hindered by the capacity of the markets. Many, if not most, money managers are locked into quarterly comparisons of performance that prevent a longer view and focus on managing many issues. The field of play for the smaller speculator therefore is not often occupied by predatory competitors seeking to destroy him.

Smaller *speculative* traders can use their advantage on execution to fully exploit market swings. They can nimbly add positions on the way up or down, bail out at the peak or bottom, reverse or go into trading range mode until another trend is established. Moreover, they can add positions on pullbacks, as well as fade the trend during excesses of the advance or decline—times when you must be particularly nimble. The result is more profit opportunities that arise from more comprehensively exploiting market movement.

That said, it's not possible to constantly be right on a moving market. Most objective trading schemes are tied to one mode: trending behavior. That's because the most spectacular gains appear to come from catching a big ride. Surely, you must sit through a lot of small moves that don't turn into trends, but you plan to be there when the big one shows up. You hope that the move will be big enough to cover all the losses and indecisive trades.

To take full advantage of the market's movements, to extract all the energy available in the tide of the price cycle (ultimately the business cycle), we need to employ the tactics of today and the next three weeks while keeping in mind the strategy for the next six months to a year and the grand swing over the next four or five years. This book emphasizes that task up to about six months.

The key to this is determining which mode we're in and employing an objective trading strategy for that mode. Being objective means we know for each tactic in each strategy what winning trades or losing trades look like, and therefore how much capital to use and where to cut our losses. Oddly, just about any trading rule that objectively specifies an entry and exit serves our purpose.

Once we have objective means of defining trade modes, taking trades, and managing losses, we should trade all the time, not just on a single trading rule. A strong set of rules should allow us to be active in all market phases. I refer to this continuous activity as a campaign, a concerted effort to build capital.

Finally, I hope to keep things simple. This isn't the book for exotic definitions of trend or piles of theoretical mathematics, because the state of the art doesn't support such approaches. I hope most traders will be able to follow my argument by first looking at the pictures, then reading the text. Footnotes will lead to other references, sources, and products. I'll achieve my purpose here if I show a comprehensive view of recording and exploiting market behavior.

THE BIG PICTURE

What if we could extract from the market every bit of profit that its fluctuations allow? We'd be pretty excited, right? Even if we could get to half of it, we'd be pumped up. After all, the market is constantly moving somewhere, but we all know how difficult it is to be there and be right. Few of us have the agility or the market sense to constantly and consistently ride the waves and wavelets in the right direction.

Yet what we ask isn't crazy. We *should* be working toward that goal, even if we can't make it.[1] Instead, what typically happens is that we lock into a single mode of trading or a single trading "system," typically a trend-following mechanism. If there's no trending or the trend we seek isn't behaving the way our system likes to see things, we're in for trouble. If we do get headed in the right direction and at the right time, we don't have a way to fully exploit the advance or decline we're riding. How do we know when to add positions and when to take them off?

Then, when we reach the end of the trend—what to do? Most systems (all the ones I've seen) just bail out and wait for another setup like the one they are programmed to see. There's no thought of reversing into the countertrend, no plan to exploit a hiatus at a new level. Most so-called trading systems are one-note affairs.

This single-minded approach may have some virtue, but it limits us when we most need to make hay—when things are going right. We know we're going to have the numerous small losses—we need to make a ton when there are fish in the water. A one-note trading rule doesn't do it no matter how many setups, triggers, and filters we tack onto it. That's just going for the perfect entry, the unreachable Valhalla of retail traders.

Instead, see the whole picture (see Figure 1.1), not just the uptrend. Look at the basing, the trend, the reversal, and the ranging, which are not, as we know, the only possible sequence. Instead of a

---

[1] To get a taste of this, check the "perfect indicator" in MetaStock for Windows and DOS by Equis International. The indicator is used as a reference, not a trading signal.

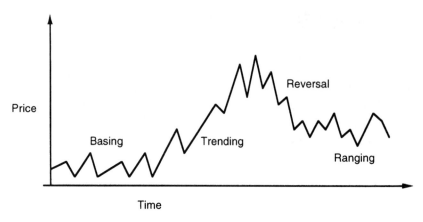

FIGURE 1.1   THE WHOLE CAMPAIGN. Instead of looking just for trends, plan for an entire campaign of trades, some exploiting ranging and some exploiting trending.

single tactical fight over a single entry and exit on the trend, consider a whole campaign of tactical conflicts beginning with quiet skirmishing during a basing period, skirmishing that builds and builds until it erupts in a breakout and we commit greater and greater amounts of capital. Even within this battle—uptrend or downtrend—there are entries and exits and more skirmishes, until we sense, through heavy contact and diminishing advances, that the trend is ending.

Our campaign strategy shifts to exiting the positions we've accumulated, not in a spasmodic ejection, but carefully, conceding ground while considering the possibility of a complete reversal of trend—and our position. Or perhaps ground gained will be held and we can go into defensive positions, hacking back and forth around support and resistance, holding a ridgeline, in combat terms, with aggressive patrolling and probing assaults.

The combat terminology isn't meant to indicate that we analyze or think in these terms but only to suggest the overall picture. Obviously, there's plenty of colorful but unquantifiable verbiage we could use to describe these concepts. I want you to campaign using objective, *quantifiable* tools. This book will illustrate how to campaign using New York Light Crude as an example.

BASICS

A young basketball player is fascinated with The Shot. He doesn't think about the footwork he needs to get to the shot. He's not aware of position on the court or even body position in the constant tactical encounters at each end of the court. These fundamentals can make for easy buckets or, alternatively, the continual need to pull a great shot out of nowhere time after time. (As a trader, which mode would you prefer?)

Neither is the young player aware of the substitution pattern, game pace, or matchups except as he faces them momentarily on the court or while sitting on the bench. The game plan is completely subordinate to hitting the shot and not getting beaten to the hoop.

It is the same in trading: There are some basics and there are tactical engagements within the endless campaign. To start with the basics, let's talk about time and loss.

Time Horizon

This clumsy term refers to the period of time you consider when trading, time past (for analysis) and the future (for projections). You need to know if your horizon is thirty seconds, thirty days, or thirty months. Many analytical techniques need to be given the number of days (or minutes or months) they should include in their calculations. Charts inevitably select a certain time period. Is it just the past ten days that are relevant to tomorrow's price, or the past six weeks or ten years? Technical analysts argue that the market in some sense remembers past prices, that past prices have an impact on today's price and tomorrow's. Well, then, what's the relevant memory span?

To answer this, there are both theory and practice. In true theory, that rigorously maintained by academics, the market has little memory. Studies of autocorrelation of returns have almost all shown little evidence of today's return being significantly related to yesterday's, let alone that of several weeks, months, or years ago.[2] Although the distribution of returns isn't quite normal, the difference from normal is of interest only to academicians, options players, and arbitrageurs with very sophisticated analytical and execution capabilities. As for the question of market memory, the efficient markets school didn't find evidence of it.

Nevertheless, it's hard to think of a market that trades independently of previous prices, that is, at $25 one day, $84 the next, $2 the next, and $5,000 the next. If returns are statistically random, what order is it that we see in charts? How are prices related to each other over time? Despite our abysmal ignorance of how markets truly work, there have been some suggestions that have merit.

Statistics

Evidence of order in the markets came from Cliff Sherry[3] in the 1980s, when he pointed out that our conventional statistical analysis might be misleading us. In his first book, Dr. Sherry asked whether financial time series were truly random, independent, and stationary. He provided techniques for determining first stationarity (whether the rules for creating prices were changing or not); then dependence (whether prior prices have any impact on current prices); and then randomness (whether today's price or the change in price is a coin toss). In applying the techniques to real-world data such as the S&P 500, he found data that were indeed stationary, contained serial dependencies, but evidenced random price changes. In most trading within a certain temporal window, past prices have an impact on future prices, *but* within that range of dependence, price changes occur randomly.

---

[2] Paul Cootner, *The Random Character of Stock Prices* (Cambridge: MIT Press, 1964).

[3] Clifford J. Sherry, *The Mathematics of Technical Analysis* (Chicago: Probus, 1992).

I mention all this because the idea of a temporal window pops up again and again in trading. The market's "memory" is not indefinite, but it exists and is worth studying. Hence, the study of cycles, the use of averages, and the setting of parameters for time in indicators all have some substantive basis. You could legitimately use the evidence of dependence when characterizing the market you're trading. If you found that 21 days was about right for the S&P (or 200 days), you'd include that much data in your data files (at a minimum) and construct your indicators, cycles, and charts with that number in mind.

Cycles

One approach to estimating a specific time horizon is to pick out cyclic behavior in prices. Anyone familiar with trading literature will have seen analyses based on astrological cycles, Gann precepts, seasonal factors, and so forth. I propose we give these techniques their due without indulging in them. The inability to objectively define and test their precepts makes them unsuitable for broad usage whatever their validity.

However, beginning with Hurst[4] in 1970 and continuing fitfully in trading literature since, a line of thought has developed that attempts to define mathematically the cyclic content, if any, in market price streams ("streams" as in streams of data). Engineers, in particular, have been energetic in this regard, and two techniques, Fourier transforms[5] and maximum entropy spectral analysis (MESA)[6] have proven consistently applicable.

---

[4] J. M. Hurst, *The Profit Magic of Stock Transaction Timing* (Englewood Cliffs: Prentice-Hall, 1970).

[5] Anthony W. Warren and Jack K. Hutson, "Fast Fourier Transform," *Technical Analysis of Stocks and Commodities,* vol. 1 (Seattle: Technical Analysis, Inc., 1981). I don't recommend this technique: MESA is much better at extracting short-term cycles using short data lengths.

[6] Anthony W. Warren, "An Introduction to Maximum Entropy Method (MEM) Technical Analysis," *Technical Analysis of Stocks and Commodities,* vol. 2 (Seattle: Technical Analysis, Inc., 1982). See also John Ehlers's work based on a Ph.D. the-

The result has been that cyclic content, at least insofar as we can capture it mathematically, is episodic. John Ehlers, easily the leading analyst in this area, reports realistically that depending on the item being traded and, probably, many other factors we don't know about, sharply defined cyclic content pops up between 20% and 30% of the time. The good news from my experience is that when it does pop up, it usually centers around consistent values—numbers of days being the most common measure (see Figure 1.2).

Practically speaking, this means that it is possible to make an educated guess about the relevant time frame for your analysis. For Treasury bonds, this value has almost imperceptibly expanded from eight days in 1982 to around ten days in the past 13 years. If I must make a guess or supply a parameter for bonds (say, for a moving average or an RSI), I'd use ten with great comfort. Other futures contracts show similar phenomena. I rarely trade stocks, but my cursory experience is that stocks exhibit stable cyclic content in about the same proportions. After surveying the Dow 30 on May 9, 1995, using Ehlers's software MESA, I found that about one-third showed a consistent level of cyclic content during the previous four months.

The value you use will change and MESA makes estimating these values visually easy. At the same time, you will also be able to judge from the smearing of the spectrum how reliable the estimate is. Plus, the lack of cyclic content may be an important clue that trending behavior has set in. Figure 1.3 shows an even clearer example from the Commodity Research Bureau's index.

Economic Cycles

More difficult to apply while seaching for time horizons in speculative trading are the economic cycles that I, among many, find relatively consistent. Whole foundations[7] are devoted to chronicling

sis by John Parker Burg, Stanford University, 1975. John F. Ehlers, *MESA and Trading Market Cycles* (New York: John Wiley & Sons, Inc., 1992).

[7] Foundation for the Study of Cycles, 900 W. Valley Road, Suite 502, Wayne, PA 19087. Phone (610) 995-2120, FAX (610) 995-2130. Columbia Center for Interna-

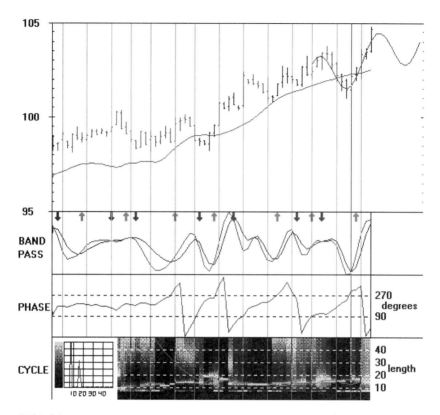

FIGURE 1.2 EXEMPLARY MESA ANALYSIS. During early 1995, the Treasury bond futures' dominant cycle (the bottom panel in the display) oscillates between 8 and 15 days. The cursor shows a day with a subpeak at 12 days. Cyclic content is high during periods when the line in the bottom panel has no (or little) color smeared above and below it. A sharply defined peak in the spectral display to the left is the result.

the components of economic expansion and contraction. Many business folk have a ground-level view of this through their daily interactions and are especially aware of it after they've been through it once or twice. Local banks are usually in the business of

tional Business Cycle Research, Columbia University, 645 Madison Avenue, 19th floor, New York, NY 10022. Phone (212) 688-2222. National Bureau of Economic Research, 1050 Massachusetts Avenue, Cambridge, MA 02138. Phone (617) 868-3900.

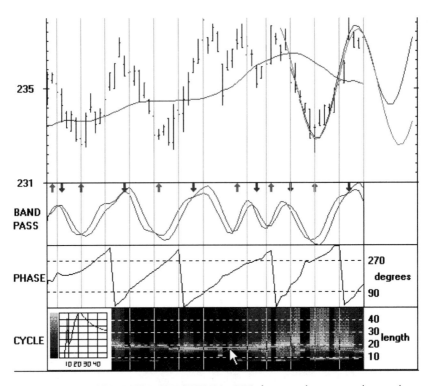

FIGURE 1.3   CRB MESA SPECTRUM. CRB futures show a rock-steady cyclic content of 20 days during early 1995 in the cycle bar at the bottom of the display. Note the sharply defined spectral curve peaking at 20 days with a subpeak at half-cycle length around 9 days.

structuring themselves for an interest rate outlook that ebbs and flows with the economy. Either of these sources is better than general journalistic coverage, which usually comes after the fact and is focused on today's economic reports.

For a trader's purposes, business cycles are primarily setups for short-term trades. It helps, for example, to know when cyclical stocks are likely to respond to expansions and, generally, to know which way interest rates are likely to go as the economy moves. Rotation into and out of industry groups is a full-time practice for some portfolio managers, and even futures traders can exploit the differing performances of grand sectors (equities, debt, currencies, and commodities) with all the vehicles now available.[8]

Finding a trading horizon with economic cycles requires pockets deep enough for a one- to two-year swing. An active speculative trader will likely have more immediate opportunities come up during that length of time than he or she can ignore, opportunities that won't require committing a lot of margin money to accumulating a position that won't be disbursed for four years. For example, the usual result is that a speculative trader may be aware of copper basing at low values for a year or so, but won't take positions until short-term factors indicate a break upward.

Charting Averages

Every investor, trader, or speculator knows that at some point the trade he or she has in mind will be ready to go. The only question is what action will cause the trader to take action. Waiting for a breakout in an undervalued stock is simply waiting for the other people at the market to recognize what you see. Assuming you can't buy all the stock and realize its true value by selling it or grabbing the cash flow from it (i.e., a takeover), you must to have public opinion on your side to realize the value of the company, or the commodity, or the instrument. Since cash talks, nothing indicates the concurrence of opinion better than other people paying up for a tradable and thereby causing the price to move.

It's at this point that technical analysis serves to define breakout, define movement, and define our time horizon. The most venerable of the technical tools, moving averages, probably does the job best. Having the virtues of simplicity and an inability to ignore a trend, averages that give reasonable crossings of price channels and skim tops and bottoms nicely can be defined visually simply by plotting

---

[8] To home in on these, Martin Pring's *Intermarket Review* serves futures traders well with practically rigorous criteria for defining different points in economic cycles. Martin Pring, "Intermarket Review," P.O. Box 624, Gloucester, VA 23061-0624. Phone (800) 221-7514.

the averages and adjusting them to fit. You'll find an amazing concurrence in length with the values generated through analytical techniques like MESA. We will examine this further in Chapter 2.

Summarizing Time

Having an idea of the cycle time or response rate of a tradable helps in defining indicators, building trading strategies, and selecting trading instruments. Given the roughness of the data, the tools I have described will serve well.

Loss—Not Risk

The second basic skill is losing money minimally. An aphorism states the cardinal rules of trading as "First, don't lose your money. Second, see rule one." One must be more artful to avoid losing money than to make money. Not losing money is also the key to winning the investment game. Especially in futures where, absent commissions, the game is zero-sum, you must minimize the size of your largest loss. My approach to success is not on good trading signals but on minimizing losses.

So, let's not use the word "risk" because, quantitatively, it refers to the variance of returns, and variance could be a gain as well as a loss. What we fear is loss. What we must minimize is loss.

Fine, but how? You need to know what kind of situation your trading rule selects and the usual results. Necessarily, the market will do one of three things with your position: advance it, ignore it, or go against it. Whatever your entry rule, you—like all traders—must know when to admit you're wrong and turn around.

I take the approach of observational experience. Given a consistent rule, I ask how winning trades behave and how losing trades behave. I'll show by example that winning trades just don't go very far bad. If a trade does go bad by a certain amount, *an amount you can measure*, it's probably time to get out or reverse your position. This is how you avoid losing excessively and, thereby, how you win.

If we have this information—we know what we will lose on a losing trade—simulation (another form of experience) or historical testing can tell us what our odds of winning and losing are, and the two (probability and expected outcome) give us our capital requirement.[9] Exercises like this have generated the rule of thumb that any given loss should be no more than 2%[10] of one's total capital, though active traders vary that number as low as 1% and as high as 5%.

With our time horizon and loss level in hand, we're ready to campaign.

CAMPAIGNING

Take it as a given that the market is either moving or it's not. I use only two modes, trending or nontrending, despite entire catalogues of chart patterns that encapsulate differing behaviors.[11] This simplification leaves us to deal only with periods of quiet and periods of trending (see Figure 1.4).

The point of campaign thinking is to exploit the full range of market behavior for profit rather than to lock into a single mode of trading, whether it be waiting for a trend to assert itself, trading into ranges, or trading oscillators. In a campaign, as contrasted to

---

[9] Nauzer J. Balsara, *Money Market Strategies for Futures Traders* (New York: John Wiley & Sons, Inc., 1992), pp. 8–22.

[10] I picked this number out of the air early in my career, and I'm now at a loss to defend it with a reference to anything back then. It turns out to be in the ballpark for a very low risk of ruin. Balsara's book doesn't check below 10%, but see testing reported by Tom Basso in "The Trader's Psyche: Tom Basso," *Technical Analysis of Stocks and Commodities*, vol. 11, p. 451. Another practical reference is from Monroe Trout at 1.5% in Jack Schwager, *The New Market Wizards* (New York: HarperCollins, 1992), p. 167.

[11] Robert D. Edwards and John Magee, *Technical Analysis of Stock Trends,* 6th ed. (Boston: John Magee Inc., 1992). For candlestick patterns, refer to, Steve Nison, *Japanese Candlestick Charting Techniques* (New York: New York Institute of Finance, 1991). Also, see Steve Nison, *Beyond Candlesticks* (New York: John Wiley & Sons, 1994).

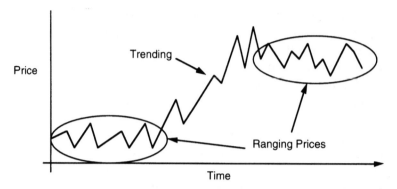

FIGURE 1.4 TRENDING OR RANGING? In this book, I use a simple two-mode description of market behavior. Although there are far more complex conceptions (for example, Elliott waves or cyclical models), to make the point of analyzing market behavior using our experience, only this simple model is needed.

the typical single-mode approach, we must alter our stance as the market gives us clues, make entries, lose lightly on some trades (maybe the majority), win on others, reverse into the proper mode, add positions as fortune favors us, and exit or reverse the entire position as the chance occurs (see Figure 1.5).

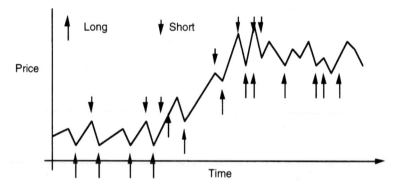

FIGURE 1.5 CAMPAIGN TRADING. Don't take these idealized entries too seriously—nothing ever goes like this. Instead, consider the greater number of opportunities to build a position with an approach that exploits all modes of market behavior.

Clearly, a single trading rule—the usual approach in published trading systems—is inadequate for this constant thrust and parry. We'll need several rules, several ways of looking at the market and judging what mode we're in and how to exploit it.

Whatever mode the market is in, the trader must have a position in order to profit and to build the position to profit more. Many trading strategies assume that a one-contract strategy can be scaled up if successful. Were all the opportunities presented by market movement exploited, many more initial entry techniques would be seen to be valuable. For example, a trend entry by itself might happen barely enough times to offset many small false entries. If, in addition to the initial entry, other entries could be made profitably in concert with the first, a barely profitable technique would be seen as only the first step in a series of trades of much greater value.

Of course, achieving this is not easy, but the argument that a single trading strategy is the way to approach the market must be suspect—if only because we are aware of all the amazing behaviors the market shows us given the millions of actions that impinge it. We cannot fathom all that, but we really have only two dimensions with which we must deal: up-down and time. From these simplicities, we must insert an opportunistic series of trades that probe for what the market will give us, trades with the overall goal of creating a profitable position from very comfortable levels.

CLASSIC STAGES

Basing, breakout, trending, topping, and retreat: these form the classic stages of a market campaign. The crude oil market, while not as clear cut as the bond market from which I abstracted the campaign image, has moments of drama of its own (see Figure 1.6).

My sense is that markets trade differently, reacting more or less violently and more or less continuously to change. Charts capture this sense of distinction by showing the rapidity of advance or decline, the gaps, the range about points of value, and the dependency (or lack of it) on past pricing. If markets trade distinctly (though interrelationships obviously exist), our general approach

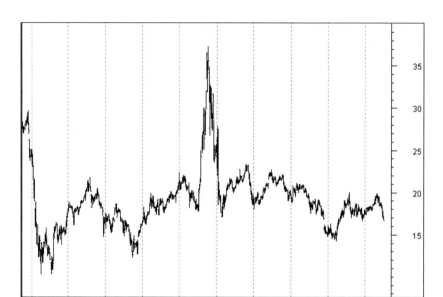

FIGURE 1.6   ACTION IN CRUDE. New York Light Crude hasn't moved as violently as, say, Treasury bonds in this decade, but Crude has had its moments. The huge size of the energy markets gives prices fair continuity for trading purposes.

must master this variety rather than impose a spurious consistency such as "a good trading system should do well in every market." I'm going to show you an analysis of New York Light Crude,[12] but only the analytics will carry over to other markets, not the results.

Mode 1: Trading Range

The ideal setup for a campaign is when a market is quiet, going nowhere. This is when it's never mentioned in the market press, volume is low and regular, and there's not much activity at the specialist's desk or in the pit or on the phones. Everyone knows the bid-

---

[12] I rarely trade Crude. I selected it to see how my techniques would apply to something besides rates and currencies.

ask spread and attempts to push it, just to earn rolling eyes and sarcastic comments. On the screens, it doesn't screen. It never sets off anyone's search criteria, usually oscillating about some central value. Its regression is a flat line for any tradable horizon, its averages trundle through the daily range bars, and daily range itself is historically small.

During this period, we'd like to trade into the trading range. The major concern is whether there is enough of a trading range to trade. We need a range roughly twice the loss we're going to take on breakout.

Loss? On breakout? You see, the plan is to trade into (or "across," if you prefer) the range. Therefore, by definition, when the breakout comes, we'll be going the wrong way, necessitating a reverse. If the range we've just come across is 18 points and we're going to lose 18 points on the breakout, we'll just be even. Better would be to get ahead by 18 to 36 points coming across the range, but of course this is determined by the market you're in.[13] Some markets will allow you more than others when they are in a range.

We'll develop the specifics of this strategy later. For now, the campaign begins with a quiet period. As we oscillate back and forth across the range, we gradually build up our position and build it profitably. We'll give up some of those profits when we break out—how much is unknown but, as we'll see, experience may give us some guides.

We may not have a long time to exploit this quiet time. In stocks, it could be years; in agricultural commodities, it's partially dictated by the season and partly dictated by the reactive cycles of the producers; in the hard commodities, the economic cycles seem to dictate what's moving and how long we have to accumulate when there's no movement. In financials, quiescent periods were very short during the 1970s and 1980s, but the increasing firmness and consistency of the monetary authorities in the 1990s is dampening market volatility and increasing the length of quiescence. On the other hand, the huge amounts of money flogging about the globe for short-term return and speculative adventure has shortened the waiting periods in currencies dramatically. Long famous for their

---

[13] For Crude, the range will be about 100 trading points and the loss about 30.

tendency to trend, currencies are now major speculative vehicles for their depth, liquidity, and constant movement.

Each person will pick the time frame within which he or she speculates. Those wishing no overnight losses will trade intraday. Those trading positions will be anywhere from two days to several months. We can look at daily or weekly data.[14] For the purposes of this book, we'll use interday pricing and let the market dictate how long we're in any given trade, just as it dictates how long we're in any ranging or trending modes.

Trending

The very best trades never go wrong. A wonderful reaffirmation of the underlying justice of the world (for a trader) is a trade that is profitable thirty seconds after it's put on and never looks back. Most likely, it's a trend trade, one associated with a steady advance or decline in pricing, though it could be something that meanders in a slightly profitable zone.

A one-note trading strategy will usually find this situation and ride it. That's fine. That's progress, but there's more to be done. We'd like to extract every bit of profit that's coming to us and the way toward that in a trend is to pile on. The questions are "Where?" and "When?"

Briefly, "where" means continuously during the advance and "when" is when prices are cheap or dear during an advance or decline. I believe these verbal rules can be executed objectively by referring to your experience with the market and Chapter 5 is devoted to this topic, but for now take it that a period of trending is a time for working, not just waiting.

Not that waiting is bad. It was LeFèvre[15] who said he made most of his money waiting. Once you have your positions, you do

---

[14] I don't mention monthly data because I've never run into anyone actually trading from it.

[15] Edwin LeFèvre, *Reminiscences of a Stock Operator* (Burlington, Vt.: Fraser Management Associates, 1980), p. 68. The full quote is "I want to tell you this: It

wait. However, in the campaign mode, you must constantly seek new positions using a variety of entry criteria. Like an infantry company commander, you're always patrolling your front, probing. During a trend, it's the same.

Breaking Out

Actually getting to a trend from a trading range is a little tough. First of all, under my scheme, you've been trading back into the range, so to get right with the new trend you have to take a loss and reverse.

Perhaps more difficult (because the trade could be executed mechanically by an executing broker) is reversing your mindset. I won't dwell on psychology in this book (though I'm not above referring to the phenomena all traders know),[16] but you should know that it's because I found it nearly impossible to decisively reverse my own opinion that I had to develop a trading system that could be mechanically implemented. I'm in awe of traders who can, on their internal fortitude, see they're wrong and get right. I found out early that I wasn't one of them, and just about everything you see in this book is the result of an effort to get my snap judgment out of the way of making money. I hope to show you a way where your judgment in analyzing experience can lead to mechanical rules for analysis and execution.

Perhaps reversing with a loss won't seem so bad to you if you've had the good fortune to be trading a range and just traded profitably across the range to your breakout point. If, say, your range is 90 points, you've built up a profit over what turned out to

---

never was my thinking that made big money for me. It always was my sitting. Got that? My sitting tight!"

[16] See Jake Bernstein, *The Investor's Quotient*, 2d ed. (New York: John Wiley & Sons, Inc., 1993) for as good a treatise on trading psychology as I've seen. Also, Alexander Elder's mantra, "I am a trader. I have it within me to do great harm to my trading account" is worth keeping in mind. See Alex Elder, *Trading for a Living* (New York: John Wiley & Sons, Inc., 1993).

actually be the start of a trend at the bottom of the range. If, on the other hand, you've just gone from a downtrend to an uptrend, you will cash in your profit from the previous trend and immediately reinvest in the new move.

Adding Positions on the Trend

Once we're into a trend (and the best early indicator is the entry trade that never went bad), it's time to add positions in the right direction. The best place is when prices are cheap or dear relative to the advance or decline measure (in this book, a short, moving average). Others use trend lines or trading bands. Waves of advance may be as small as stairsteps or as pronounced as retracements, but if we're genuinely into a sustained advance the underlying channel can be marked out using averages, trading bands, regressions, or trend lines. I prefer averages, simply because they can't go wrong and, in my experience, they have been consistent over the past 12 years.

Use an average that skims tops and bottoms of declines or advances. You'll probably find the length of the average is remarkably similar to the cyclical content of the data series.[17] All you really need to know, however, is that one characteristic or element of experience that tends to define the trading channel for you during advances or declines. You're free to set it as tightly as you like. Just keep in mind that when prices decline to an advancing average during a trend, your buy order will be waiting for them.

On the other side of the channel, prices will be genuinely frothy. If people are paying up or selling out at an extreme, prices must be dear or cheap. If dear, let's sell some things we bought cheaply; if cheap, let's buy some things we sold higher. Caution: Don't drop your underlying position. Whether you've kept it constant since trend entry or have added to it, just squeeze out the add-on trades you took as the price fluctuated about its line of trend.

---

[17] John Ehlers: quoted in John Sweeney, "Back to Averages," *Technical Analysis of Stocks and Commodities* (Seattle: Technical Analysis, Inc., April, 1991), p. 98.

Ending the Trend

Just as I was not worried about the "optimal" trading rule, I'm not worried about your exit. As long as the exit rule is specified going in, we can observe the actual gains and losses from the trading strategy, which means we can control losses and thus end up winning.

It's unrealistic to shoot for the top price in an uptrend. That's not going to happen except by a statistical fluke (the price extreme probably has a volume of one). At the top, as all along the way, traders are oscillating about some changing concept of value, searching for levels that will generate transactions. Who knows what has changed in the fundamental world, if anything? You're probably not privy to it or aware of it. Folks who are privy wonder if what's changed will make a difference. The uncertainty is resolved by sheer weight of numbers and the timing of actions taken by disparate traders. When that weight shows itself in price reversal, it's time to act.

The issue for the campaigner is whether the reversal is simply a reaction in a trend, a reversion to trading range, or a complete reversal of trend. Only the price's action can ultimately tell, and in the process of fighting over this terrain, more tactical loses will be taken, eating up some of the gains from the trend. The basic clue will be violation of the theory we had before: that advancing trending prices should be roughly contained along the lines of our advance, whether those lines are trend lines, averages, or whatever method you use. It is the violation of the previous theory that tells us change has occurred, not (or, rarely) fundamental news.

Reversing the Trend—Return to Ranging

Unless you're trading something that trends with the economic cycles (one reason I like currencies, rates, and indices), the most likely outcome after a trend is reversion to trading range activity, particularly in stocks where truly new information is scarce. Having no new ideas, traders pushing the price around are unlikely to take it anywhere and newcomers to the issue are few. There's simply a lack of interest.

Once the trending theory has been violated, the question is whether true trend reversal or range trading is next. Here again, look to experience. Study the typical ranging of the market you're trading. Bonds, if you had to pick a number, would probably flutter up and down about three points. At the bottom of this expected range, we can take a low-loss stand. If correct, we have a great entry into the range. If not, we have another trend (because both our previous trend theory and the range theory have been shown incorrect) into which we reverse.

To apply concrete rules to this generic approach (and there could be many rules), we'll simply use the price's crossing and recrossing of our short-term average. Amplified later, we'll see that this simple approach can find the ranges we seek.

ANOMALIES

Broadening Ranges

One experience that this approach cannot handle is a broadening range, one example of which came up in late 1994 (see Figure 1.7). A broadening range is simply wider and wider oscillations about a presumably nonexistent value point. Here, it's gone beyond shooting for stops at either end of the range to genuine confusion as melee after melee produces higher highs and/or lower lows within the time frame we trade. At each extreme, my campaigner will reverse into trend mode taking a loss, only to reverse back into the range taking another loss. Although some of the loss will be made up traversing the range, discipline will be tested severely and financing strained.

Fortunately, broadening ranges are rare. There is no protection from them that I can recommend, and we must trade them—we must have a position if we are to profit—with the financing to absorb them.

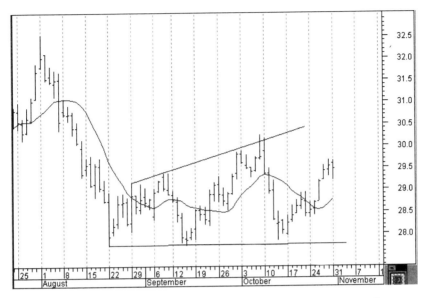

FIGURE 1.7   BROADENING RANGE. The trending-ranging market model breaks down when broadening chart formations occur. Here one pops up in late 1994.

SUMMARY

The classic campaign was one of accumulation through distribution. A mass of longs or shorts was built up and then disbursed to the crowd at more favorable prices. In the 1920s all the longs and shorts were held together analytically. No distinction was made between the management of the first trade and the management of the fifth, which was brought on later, sometimes far into the campaign. Additional trades often have distinctive characteristics that can be observed, categorized, and exploited. It makes much more sense to treat them this way than to pyramid or blindly bump up one's position.

In contrast to the old-style campaign, I advocate a continuous campaign using market indicators to specify the mode we're in, loss-control techniques to generate profitability even when our trading signals aren't God-given, and varying tactics to compound our position.

To do this, the first innovation is measuring everything from the point of entry your trading rules specify for the market mode you're in. This puts all decisions in the domain of price movement from entry.

The second is the technique of measuring adverse excursion and favorable excursion from the point of entry: how far winning trades and losing trades go against you or for you. Measuring adverse excursion allows you to manage the discrete positions accumulated during a campaign of trading. This way, add-on trades in a trend will have a different expectation of loss/gain/duration[18] than the first trend trade. More generally, each tactic of the campaign will have different trading characteristics that can be defined by the behavior of the trades using that tactic, behavior that is characterized using the measurements of adverse and favorable excursion.

Everyone trading, particularly those adding positions, is nervously aware that the market is constantly switching modes (or faking a switch). The usual response is to sell out the whole budding position on the first adverse twitch, curtailing profits. Alternatively, nerves of steel are invoked to hold the position.

That our business is to be determined by the emotional stability of the trader is unacceptable. Instead, look at the characteristics of the trade taken: its price excursions, its rate of advance, and its duration. These characteristics tell you what, if anything, to do other than wait. Now we can begin to manage trades quantitatively (though not formulaically), a practice that I regard as a major step forward from the usual bromides, whatever their truth.

The Argument from Experience

In this book, I innovate not originate. Practical traders have had these techniques in their guts for centuries. The innovation is in

---

[18] *Duration* as used here refers to the time of the trade, not the relation between a bond's price change and the change in its yield to maturity.

measuring specific experience to "mechanize" the definition of loss/ reversal points. We need to find experience-based price levels where stands can be taken with minimal loss exposure until the overall trend or range becomes apparent. I say to measure the behavior of the market from your entry points, consistently taken, and use that experience as your guide.

Isn't this what "experience" has been for centuries? A trader takes a trade. Something happens. He takes another. Something happens. He trades; the market responds, again and again. In his subconscious (or in his trading diary) patterns of behavior start to form, his behavior and the market's in relation to his entries. "Given my tactic, this is what happens when things go right, that happens when things go wrong," he mumbles to himself. He isn't doing anything glamorous, just accumulating experience.

Is it realistic to think that something of this real-world experience can be captured and exploited more systematically? Let me show you one way.

2
Trading the Trend

I begin with trading trends because it's the idea most people use when campaigning: getting on board the big move. For our purposes, catching the trend is just one part of the overall campaign, albeit a major part, but catching a long move is clear in everyone's mind: we get in low or high, wait, ride it, and get out high or low.

An example of trading a trend should allow me to introduce some other ideas I'll use throughout the book. These ideas include finding time horizons, defining market modes (trending or non-trending), measuring adverse and favorable price movement, setting stops, and managing trades. Each of these is easier to see in the context of a trend trade. Having seen them used within a trend trade, we can more easily apply them to trades in trading ranges, add-on trades, or reversal trades.

TRENDS

Before discussing trading ranges or trends, we should really discuss trends that go nowhere, as well as those that go somewhere. Here I'm using "trend" in the general sense of prices persistently going down, up, or sideways. This isn't the normal approach, so keep it in mind. We 'see' a pattern when prices on a chart persis-

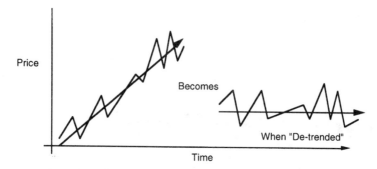

FIGURE 2.1   TREND TO FLAT TREND. Our term "trend" usually refers to persistent movement up or down, but it could also refer to persistent movement sideways. A trading range is a flat trend.

tently go in one direction rather than another. This 'persistence' accounts for much of the 'behavior' that we recognize intuitively when looking at a chart and many of the ideas people have for trading. So I try to keep in mind that what I perceive visually and what I try to work out mathematically may not be the same thing at all (see Figure 2.1).

The idea of trend really involves the ideas of persistency and consistency, for want of better terms. Let's call the *direction of change* of price "consistency" and the *duration* of that consistent change "persistency." Just as Gann would reportedly have had it, trend is perceived by the attributes of *price* (consistent price change) and *time* (continuing consistent price change).

That persistence[1] involves time is the most difficult part for people to grasp, but it's easiest to just imagine, to begin with, three price bars (Figure 2.2). Unless they go straight up, straight down, or are completely flat, we don't perceive trend (part 1).

Add a few more bars (more evidence, more time) and we apply consistency visually (part 2). Add a few more bars (even more time)

---

[1] Persistence [MF persister, fr. L persistere, fr per-+ sistere] to take a stand, stand firm; to remain unchanged or fixed in a specified character, condition, or position. Contrast this with consistency: reliability or uniformity of successive results or events.

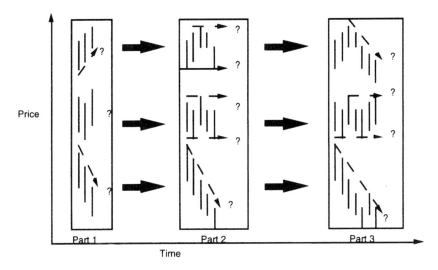

FIGURE 2.2   PERSISTENCE. The integration of events with time gives rise to our perception of trend. How much time must be involved, then, to define trend?

and we apply even more, probably broader, consistency (part 3), perhaps revising our earlier opinions. See how the mere passage of time necessarily affects our opinion? Not just that another day gives us another price bar, but the linking of the two or the evolution of price over time generates our perception.

Handling this perception as objectively and simply as possible, whether prices are going up, down, or sideways within the limits of our time frame, we're searching for and trading the same thing: consistent, persistent price action, either flat or rising and falling. Instead of using charts or fundamentals such as 10–Ks to find this sort of price action, we use quantitative indicators to identify these characteristics.

Another point: since we're always looking for the same thing, we end up trading the same way whether we're in a trading range or a trend. First, we'll trade in the direction of persistence; then we'll try to add onto that basic trade; when that fails, we'll try to reverse out of the former direction of price movement.

Objective Specification

The practical test of objectively determining trend is whether the technique can be programmed to find solutions that look good in hindsight. Ideally, the technique, whatever it is, will be practical on a day-to-day basis. Given these criteria and with no attempt to be inclusive of every idea out there, here are some of the ways people have used computers to define trend:

1. Drawing trend lines on charts. The simplest definition of a trend is higher highs and higher lows (or vice versa). Trend lines extend this idea using line. That is, they estimate where the higher lows would be in an uptrend by drawing a line somewhere along the lows already formed and extending it. In a computer, programs define pivot points,[2] track their relative price level, and draw the trend lines.[3] For an example, see Figure 2.3. And they can even define trend lines for us, as shown in Figure 2.4.

2. Defining linear regressions. The program picks up from the point the last regression broke off and begins a new regression. The new regression continues until its R^2 starts to decrease rather than increase.[4] Additional tests of slope can be added to this idea. For example, see Figure 2.5.

3. Departures from probabilistic paths. In these techniques, short-term estimates of probable future prices are defined each day based on the direction and range of prices for the

---

[2] *Pivot point* is a high or low reached in the previous *n* days. Another, older definition involves the floor trader's expected daily support and resistance levels computed from the previous day's OHLC values.

[3] Exemplary programs: Personal Analyst by Trendsetter Software, (714) 547-5005, and Advanced Get by Trading Techniques, (216) 645-0777.

[4] R^2 is a measure of the fit of a line to a series of values. As new prices appear on the chart and the regression is extended, the fit will either increase or decrease. If it increases, the new value accords well with the old values and the trend is said to continue. If it decreases, the trend may be breaking off. I heard this idea from John Ehlers, who used it in some of his early software.

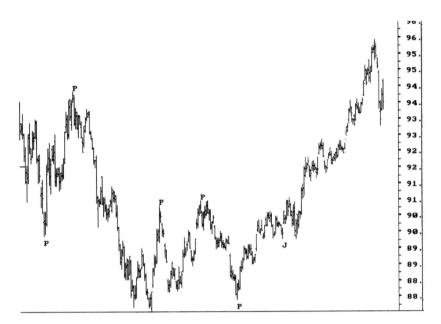

FIGURE 2.3 PIVOT POINTS. Advanced Get is one program that has the logic to select pivot points. These points are the starting gates for much further analysis.

past *n* days. The price range is used to estimate the confidence level of the forecast. An index or summary of the *n* days of predictions creates a consolidated forecast and associated confidence level. Upon excursion outside the probable range, a trend is declared and a new set of predictions begun, these defining forecast range of prices above or below current levels. An excursion outside these levels calls for a trading range to be declared.

This technique is custom-programmed and is difficult to show in a diagram, but our only purpose at this point is to list a number of ways of using programming techniques to define price movement as trending or nontrending.

4. AI tests. Rule-based logic, often referring to price-based indicators, is employed to come up with a sequence of thought

FIGURE 2.4   DRAWING TREND LINES. The lines drawn by Personal Analyst might not be those you'd draw but they do come from a consistent set of rules.

that might specify trend status. AIQ[5] is probably the most prominent retail product to do this.

5. Neural networks are trained to recognize conditions identified by humans as trending. A number of neural-net products are available to traders.[6]

6. Cyclical tests. If you assume a market that's not cycling is trending, a market that doesn't cross its trend line[7] (the price about which it is cycling) within a period of half the domi-

---

[5] AIQ Incorporated, (702) 831-2999.

[6] At this writing, probably the most convenient is NeuroShell 2 by Ward Systems Group, Inc., (301) 662-7950. More difficult to use but working further in advance is Stock Prophet by Future Wave Software, (310) 540-5373.

[7] Ehlers also developed this idea. In it, the instantaneous trend line is the simple average of the prices, but the averaging period changes from day to day as the measured dominant cycle varies. That is, as the measured cycle expands from, say, 12 days to 20 days, the number of days in the average expands from 12 to 20.

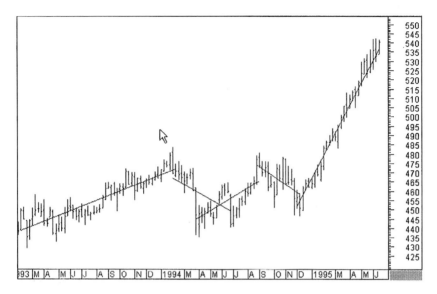

FIGURE 2.5   REGRESSION. Regression lines can be created mathematically anywhere, but given a good pivot point, a trend can be defined around one as long as R^2 does not decrease significantly.

nant cycle is trending. This can all be determined mathematically in our search for trend. A program that takes this approach is MESA, as shown in Figure 2.6.

Most trend ideas, from line drawing to regression, need a starting point. The virtue of the cyclic idea is that it doesn't need a starting point. Instead, it constantly searches the data stream for the strongest cycle present. The length of that cycle defines the look-back period and the length of the average to be used for the trend line.

Averages Again

What we've come back to, quantitatively, is an evocation of an old idea: moving averages. Without going into all the ideas behind cy-

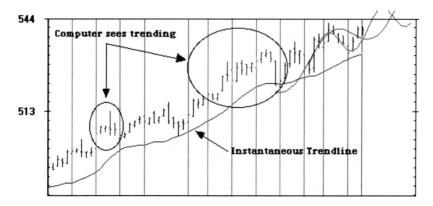

FIGURE 2.6   CYCLE TREND LINE. A cycle trend line, defined by an average of half-cycle length, can define noncyclic—hopefully, trending—behavior. Here, the machine, using MESA for Windows, sees trending after the instantaneous trend line (an average) starts upward.

cles[8] (or signal processing theory), it turns out that moving averages were a pretty good idea all along, a simple form of what engineers call a filter.[9]

Why not use the simple "price above or below" the price *n* days ago, which amounts to the same thing? Well, it turns out that averages have some other advantages. Besides being simple to calculate, averages can be applied and their length adjusted visually. Simple moving averages even have a look-back feature because you know the expiring values and thus have a clue to the average's future movement.

While you could employ quantitative techniques such as Fourier analysis or MESA to define average "length" properly, my experi-

---

[8] John J. Murphy, *Technical Analysis of the Futures Markets* (New York: New York Institute of Finance, 1986), pp. 414–455. See also John Ehlers's various articles in *Stocks and Commodities*, 1986–1988, for an explanation for laymen of the engineering approach to cycles.

[9] I'd like to report that more exotic approaches work better, but after 13 years of reviewing what's publicly available, I've seen scant improvement in trading signals from those given by averages. Perhaps proprietary techniques do better.

ence is that results are sufficiently vague (i.e., smeared spectra) and variable (peaks move constantly) that visual inspection of your charts does just as well. Although for the purposes of campaigning any consistent approach will do, averages not only provide evidence of trend but also provide opportunities for additional trades (add-on trades) during the trend.

Finally, averages can't go wrong. Even though they get whipsawed in trading ranges, it's impossible for them to miss a trend, and in trading, any element of certainty is welcome.

For example, Figure 2.7 shows a weekly chart of General Motors. A variety of averages shows different cutoffs of trend reversals and good "skimming" along tops and bottoms of trends. You, the trader, just pick visually which does the best job.

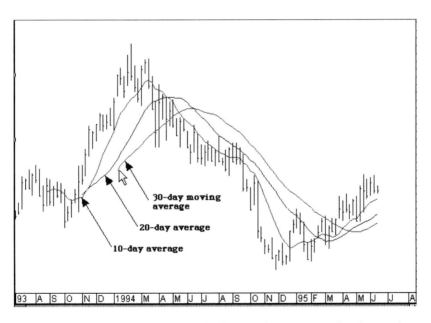

FIGURE 2.7   GM'S AVERAGES. The longer the average, the slower the definition of trend. Inspecting visually, pick the average it gives the best combination of skimming tops or bottoms, as well as reversing with trend reversals.

Skimming refers to the habit of defining the upper edge of a downtrend and the lower edge of an uptrend, given the appropriate length. This selection of length isn't perfect.[10] For one thing, some markets advance and retreat at different rates, notably bonds and other longer-term financial instruments where the mathematics of yield enhance this phenomenon. For such markets, averages of different lengths may be used, though I've rarely found this practice worthwhile. For another, volatility changes with a variety of factors affecting the "best" length. Dedicated technicians handle these factors with averages whose length adjusts to the behavior of the market,[11] but to illustrate the tactics of campaigning, simple averages will do.

For now, a trend will be in the direction in which both (1) a skimming average of a weekly chart and (2) a skimming average of the daily chart are headed up or down. Since New York Light Crude is our test bed,[12] Figure 2.8 shows an exemplary daily chart.[13]

I like to use daily charts for the short averages and weekly charts to pick up the longer average. Figure 2.9 shows a typical Crude weekly chart.[14]

The value for 12 weeks converts to 60 trading days. This is the longer average on the daily chart. Would 58 or 63 do better? I doubt we could discern much difference. The roughness of this technique would overwhelm any refinement in this number. Anyway, success won't depend on the refinement of the entry signals but on the management of losses.

---

[10] Trading bands can also define the ranges of trends, but most of these schemes also start with moving averages.

[11] See one well-done shot at this, the Variable Index Dynamic Average in Tushar Chande and Stanley Kroll, *The New Technical Trader* (New York: John Wiley & Sons, Inc., 1994), p. 49.

[12] I'm using a CSI perpetual contract here for convenience's sake. CSI and other vendors provide a variety of continuous contracts that are manufactured from the real thing to give an uninterrupted data series for analysis. I prefer the 90-day forward approximation because it gives a realistic set of daily ranges, as well as a relatively consistent tracking basis.

[13] For a weekly chart of the entire series used in this book, see the appendix.

[14] See the appendix for charts of all 11 years used in this book.

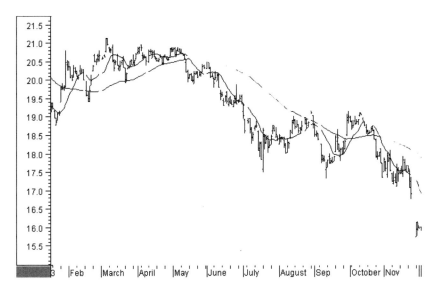

FIGURE 2.8   EXEMPLARY CRUDE. A 12-week average and a 12-day average skim tops nicely (not perfectly) and cut off trends well. Almost any rule will serve to define trend, but averages are conceptually and practically good filters.

Still, looking at the Crude charts will convince you that this two-moving-average scheme isn't perfect. The longer average skims the bottoms of the daily chart nicely three times as prices rise and one time as they fall, then plows right through the middle of a trading range between 18.0 and 19.0. The short average has similar successes and failures.

A secret number that will generate the perfect average does not exist. I've eyeballed 12 days and 12 weeks, looking for values that caught the overall price movements well, reversed as timely as a lagging average can in the great movements, and nipped along the rises and falls as neatly as I thought possible. This is pure judgement, and I'm sure others have more refined techniques. Whatever the technique, a campaigning trader simply needs rules that define the mode he or she is in, and as we'll see, averages are a serviceable tool that do that for us.

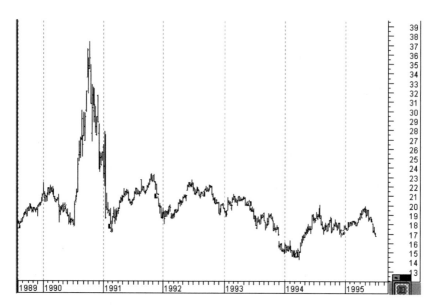

FIGURE 2.9   WEEKLY CRUDE. Over six years of widely varied price action, the 12 week (60-trading day) average does a creditable job of following prices and skimming the price channel.

TRADING RULES

In Figure 2.8, the longer average (12 weeks) converted to its daily equivalent skims along the tops and bottoms of the price movements while the daily shows nice fit, but closer. For this book, "up" is a one-period increase in an average's value and "down" is a one-period decrease in the average's value.

Our exemplary trading rule for trending will be equally simple: *If both are moving up, we go long at the close; if both down, short at the close. If in disagreement, we're out at the close.*

This simple set of trading rules has two essentials: an entry rule and an exit rule. This bounding of time by the entry date and exit date lets us define extreme price movements, both favorable and unfavorable from the point of entry. This will be important later. Plus, the two rules don't conflict. We get in when both averages are in agreement and out when one changes direction. Let's see how this works out.

EXEMPLARY TRADING

Given this simplicity, Figure 2.10 shows an equity summary for closed trades for New York Light Crude, 1984–1994, using a 12–day short average and a 12–week long average.

The summary for closed trades in Figure 2.10 does go uphill, which is good, but it's only indicative of the potential for success of this simple system because the data were perpetual data, not actual trading data. No stops are used. Experienced traders will note the runups on just a few trades and the long, slow drawdowns and flats in the equity curve. These are realistic for this type of trading system, and dealing with them is the point of inquiry for the next chapter, which gets at a key point in campaigning: managing losses.

SUMMARY

Chapter 2 has taken us from needing a trading idea to begin our campaign to a rough cut at what the results might be like. Along the way, the rationale for using simple averages has been their vi-

FIGURE 2.10   TRADING TWO MOVING AVERAGES, 1984–1994. Just a couple big winners made lots of the money here, as for most moving-average systems. The two-moving average-system also has the usual drawdowns after runups in equity.

sual convenience and the innate ability to catch trending activity (and the reverse: nontrending activity).

Campaigning starts with some such idea and usually, as I'm doing here, with the idea of catching a trend. The chart in Figure 2.10 shows that we can catch trends. Now we will explore how to play them.

3

Handling the Bad News

During any campaign, some things go well and some things go badly. The enemy makes sure of that. As it happens, a trader's enemies are literally numberless, and each can have an effect on the marketplace in which he or she trades. Therefore, it makes sense to spend a lot of time thinking about what can go wrong. Indeed, there are some traders who feel you can successfully forget putting a lot of time and effort into new entry strategies and just worry about minimizing losses. They wonder, as do I, whether you can't simply enter and exit randomly so long as you have an effective scheme of loss minimization.

This isn't the book to go into that idea, but at every stage of the campaign (or trading cycle), we must minimize our losses. I argue that the best way to analyze the problem of minimizing losses is to analyze the actual experience of losses taken in past trades.

Because so much can go wrong at any time, traders have adopted a simple approach to controlling losses: *stops*. They are the tool I'll discuss here, but I point out there are more sophisticated ways of dealing with potential losses, the easiest and most fungible of which is using *options*. Retail traders rarely take advantage of these pliable and effective instruments, and even institutional accounts may never fully employ them, but they're worth a long look when you want alternatives other than "I'm in" or "I'm out."

HOW BAD DOES IT GET?

At some point in a trade, whatever path we take becomes the wrong path for the immediate future. In trading, we are blessed with a loud, clear alarm: losing money. Even though it's easy to count and losses are reported by vast arrays of equipment second by second, losses remain tough to acknowledge. Just as it was tough when we were children to look under the bed or in a dark closet for night monsters, it's equally tough to look at a loss and acknowledge it. It was easier to hide under the covers back then, and now it's easier to adopt some defense mechanism. (The one I hear the most is "Oh, that trading rule doesn't work!" as if the entry strategy caused the loss.) To conclude, it's necessary to actually define and measure exactly what we fear: losing money.

In this book, we actually gather information on how bad things get during our trades. We'll determine whether there's any pattern in the bad news—whether there's a difference between the pattern of losing trades and the pattern of winning trades. If there is a pattern, can we exploit it? Wouldn't knowing how much adverse price movement we were in for tell us how far to hold on? And wouldn't knowing the size and frequency of our losses tell us how much money we'd need to trade a given scheme?

What about the formal definitions of risk? Although I was trained to use them, academic definitions of risk don't define the element we fear: losses. Variance is an excellent theoretical construct and commendably tractable mathematically, but the fear we have deals only with the downside of variance, not the upside. So let's look at the downside in depth.

Measuring Losses

Our operational problem is that, at some point, we must cut our loss. That point could be defined by time, by variables (other data series, judgment, or politics) independent of price, by portfolio constraints, or by financing, but usually the limit is set by the price itself. The one thing of which we are relatively sure is the price at any given moment irrespective of what is driving it. Because price is what drives our loss and we can track price, let's just measure how bad the price movement is during our winning trades. Then let's ask how bad it gets during a losing trade.

If we know anything about winning trades, it's that they end up in the black. Do they get there randomly? That is, are they at a loss one moment and, erratically, at a profit the next? This isn't our general experience (though it may seem so in the heat of an individual situation). Trades that are winners rarely go from being deep losses to overnight winners. So, if winners don't become winners erratically, is there some order to their performance?

It turns out there is. If you measure the worst price move against your position, there is a difference between that movement for winning trades and that for losing trades. Specifically, winning trades just don't have as much adverse price excursion as losing trades.

Excursion

I choose the word *excursion* pointedly because, throughout this book, I'm most interested in what the price does *from the point of entry*. I want to look at the market's behavior *in the case of* my trading action. Excursion is a neutral term that conveys neither direction nor amplitude, simply movement. Excursion also conveys that, because we don't know where price is headed, our unbiased expectation is that price will return to where it started—our entry price (see Figure 3.1).

We don't know whether there will be movement after our entry or, if there is to be movement, where, when, or how much. Excursion captures this ignorance well and, having acknowledged it, allows us to study price movement rather than ignore it.

Furthermore, when we find prices moving away from our expectation, we have evidence to suspect that something other than "noise" is causing the motion. That is, the more prices depart from our previous expectation that they would be the same tomorrow

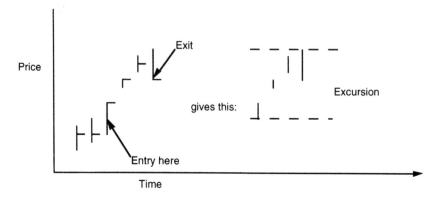

Price

Time

FIGURE 3.1   PRICE EXCURSION. Excursion refers to the movement of price from the point of entry. Usually, highs and lows are the most important in measuring favorable or unfavorable price movement.

(or perhaps oscillate lightly around today's price), the more evidence there is that our expectation was wrong and the more opportunity for profit from price change.

For now, note only that price excursion can be favorable or unfavorable, hence terminology you'll see later: *favorable excursion* (shown in Figure 3.1) or *adverse*[1] *excursion*.

What Is Maximum Adverse Excursion?

Maximum adverse excursion is the worst intraday price movement against a position at any time during the trade. For the purposes of testing, this is the high or the low of the day, keeping in mind the vagueness of these reported figures. These numbers usually have been touched only momentarily; sometimes, the actual number is even outside the reported number, which should give you some pause when relying on them. Figure 3.2 shows some examples of maximum adverse excursion (MAE),

---

[1] Adverse [ME, fr. ME *advers*, fr. L *adversus*, pp. of *advertere*] 1: acting against or in a contrary direction 2: opposed to one's interests.

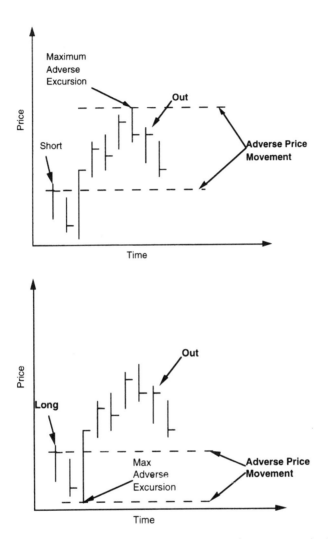

FIGURE 3.2   WHAT IS MAE? MAE (maximum adverse excursion) is the worst intraday price movement against a position measured from the point of entry. The short on the top shows the large MAE of a losing trade while the long on the bottom hits its MAE just two days after entry.

When inspecting a trading strategy visually, it's easy to pick out from the chart where the worst of the trade was. However, for purposes of analysis, it's tedious to inspect a chart, look up the low and the high, calculate the MAE, and record it. As long as you understand the idea, this is a job better left to a computer.[2]

Measuring Maximum Adverse Excursion

We're interested in measuring the adverse price movement from the point of entry. In other words, how bad does the situation get when we have a winning trade? Or a losing trade? This section lays out the mechanics of actually capturing and displaying this information.

1. *Define an entry and an exit.* Recall from Chapter 2 that our sample trading system had the following rules: go long when both averages turn up, short when both turn down, and stay out when they aren't in agreement. *Any other trading rules* can be used as long as they define the entry and the exit without stops.[3]

2. *Tabulate how far things go bad for each trade.* For each day (in this example) of each trade, calculate the worst intraday price movement, if any. If there is none, enter a zero. For long trades, use the low for the day. For shorts, use the high of the day. Table 3.1 shows an example of this method of tabulation.

   Although this method is straightforward, questions can come up. For example, what if the price first moves against the position and then moves favorably? The rule is that *MAE*

---

[2] I generally do this work on a spreadsheet because this ability has not been added to any publicly available trading software. Spreadsheet software also has great flexibility in logically defining precise trading rules, imports and organizes the data well, and usually has good graphic capabilities.

[3] This simple requirement not only lets you apply any coherent trading rules but also lets you evaluate trading systems without knowing their trading rules, just their entries and exits. Trading managers can also treat a trader in the same manner, studying his entries and exits only.

TABLE 3.1 CALCULATING MAE. A segment of the 1983 perpetual Crude contract generates a losing short position. MAE for shorts is computed as the difference between the high of each day and the entry. MAE for longs is computed using the lows.

Date	Open	High	Low	Close	Out (0) Short (–1)	Entry Price	Closed Profit or Loss	Max Adverse Excursion (MAE)	Comment
9/8/83	30.98	31.1	30.98	31.1	0	0	FALSE	FALSE	No position
9/9/83	31.02	31.11	30.95	30.96	–1	30.96	FALSE	FALSE	Go short on close, so no adverse intraday movement
9/12/83	31.01	31.03	30.81	30.82	–1	30.96	FALSE	0.07	MAE = 31.03 – 30.96
9/13/83	30.85	31.08	30.85	31.05	–1	30.96	FALSE	0.12	MAE = 31.08 – 30.96
9/14/83	30.96	31.29	30.96	31.22	–1	30.96	FALSE	0.33	MAE = 31.29 – 30.96
9/15/83	31.3	31.42	31.3	31.36	0	0	–0.4	0.46	MAE = 31.42 – 30.96

never declines. No matter what the sequence, we shall endure the worst at some point, so look for the worst that happens when we trade a specific rule set. Check each day to see if the adverse price movement has grown. (See Table 3.2 for an example of this process.)

3. *Break the trading results into winners and losers.* When you've gone through all your data, you'll have a list of trades and for each an entry, an exit, and an MAE value.[4] Next, separate the trades into two categories: winners and losers. List all the winning trades in one table and all the losing trades in another (see Table 3.3). Sophisticates can use a third category, *draws* (setting the range of profits and losses to define draws is an education in price excursion all by itself), but a third category is not necessary. Here we just need to see the difference between winners and losers, as well as see if there's a difference we can use.

4. *Tabulate the MAE for the winners and, separately, tabulate it for the losers.* To measure MAE, we'll use trading points. Dollars are just as feasible—and preferable for comparing different tradables—but to emphasize the connection of adversity to trading movement, Table 3.3 uses the actual quoted price of Crude.

5. *Sort the tabulations into categories of loss.* Here, we must address the size of the losses we can afford to take.

   We want to aggregate the actual adverse movements into chunks that will tell us something about the relation of adversity to dollar stops. For example, every adverse movement in Table 3.3 is lumped together into a unit that could be called "any size." There are ten winning trades and four losing trades with MAEs of "any size."

   If we broke up "any size" into two bins, one for MAEs less than 30 points and one for MAEs greater than 30 points, we could say, "There are three losses with MAEs under 30

---

[4] If you're setting this up as you read, you might also include the dates so you can later get data on time-in-trade.

TABLE 3.2 MAE NEVER DECLINES. MAE never declines even though price sometimes moves favorably in this 1984 example. We're looking for the worst experience at any time during the trade, and MAE measures that as hitting 30.37 on April 6, 1984, while being long at 30.62.

Date	Open	High	Low	Close	Long (1) Short (–1)	Entry Price	Closed Profit or Loss	Max Adverse Excursion (MAE)	Comment
3/28/84	30.86	30.89	30.4	30.44	0	0	FALSE	FALSE	No position
3/29/84	30.56	30.63	30.52	30.62	1	–30.62	FALSE	FALSE	Go long on close. With no adverse intra-day price movement, there's no MAE
3/30/84	30.52	30.69	30.49	30.65	1	–30.62	FALSE	0.13	MAE = 30.62 – 30.49
4/2/84	30.58	30.58	30.48	30.54	1	–30.62	FALSE	0.14	MAE = 30.62 – 30.48
4/3/84	30.53	30.62	30.53	30.6	1	–30.62	FALSE	0.14	MAE = 30.62 – 30.48
4/4/84	30.53	30.58	30.5	30.54	1	–30.62	FALSE	0.14	MAE = 30.62 – 30.48
4/5/84	30.56	30.56	30.46	30.5	1	–30.62	FALSE	0.16	MAE = 30.62 – 30.46
4/6/84	30.4	30.46	30.37	30.44	1	–30.62	FALSE	0.25	MAE = 30.62 – 30.37
4/9/84	30.4	30.49	30.4	30.42	1	–30.62	FALSE	0.25	MAE = 30.62 – 30.37
4/10/84	30.37	30.55	30.37	30.54	1	–30.62	FALSE	0.25	MAE = 30.62 – 30.37
4/11/84	30.52	30.6	30.52	30.58	1	–30.62	FALSE	0.25	MAE = 30.62 – 30.37
4/12/84	30.53	30.6	30.5	30.5	0	0	–0.12	0.25	MAE = 30.62 – 30.37

TABLE 3.3   TABULATING WINNERS AND LOSERS.

Tabulating Winners			Tabulating Losers		
Closing Date	Profit or Loss	MAE	Closing Date	Profit or Loss	MAE
7/5/83	0.09	0.07	9/15/83	−0.4	0.46
8/17/83	0.7	0.01	9/26/83	−0.04	0.08
2/14/84	1.89	0.08	4/12/84	−0.12	0.25
2/16/84	0.08	0	4/16/84	−0.02	0.02
3/16/84	0.35	0.06			
6/4/84	0.34	0			
6/12/84	0.25	0.04			
9/18/84	0.57	0.15			
9/20/84	0.05	0.07			
10/11/84	0.24	0.27			
Total:	4.56		Total	−0.58	

points," or "There is only one loss with an MAE over 30 points, trading this way." That would give us more detailed summary information. The trick is to establish whether to use 30 points or some other number.

I recommend you start from your trading capital.[5] Of that number, say $30,000, 2% should be the maximum loss on any one trade. Before we even get started, we know we'd like the stop to be no more than 2% of our capital.

Convert that 2% figure into trading points. That's the biggest bin size that would work operationally. Bigger than that and we won't be able to see if the MAEs fit our capital stop. Smaller might be helpful, though, so I recommend we take the 2% chunk size and divide it by 2. By the way, statisticians call these chunks *bins* when they're doing their work sheets. This term refers to the idea of tossing each instance or occurrence into a bin for counting.

---

[f] Be straight with yourself on this one. People tend to say, "I have $3,000, but if it's working, I'll make a lot more capital available," or sometimes, "I have $100,000 available" when they actually won't commit more than $10,000.

To summarize:

Total trading capital	$30,000
Maximum loss percentage	2%
Maximum loss in dollars	$600
Maximum loss in Crude oil trading points at $10/tick.	.6 (60 ticks)
Maximum bin size	.3 (30 ticks)

This exercise will be helpful later. If we examine the data and find that too many trades hit our stop, we can work backward from the stop level that MAE supports to the capital we'll need to trade the way we wish. Alternatively, we could conclude that we just shouldn't trade the way we tested. Many a trading idea ends right there. MAE will define your stop for you, but if it's too big for your wallet, it's telling you to forget trading the rules you used. Don't ignore this message.

6. *Sort the trades' MAEs into the bins.* We have the trades separated into winners and losers. Now we break them up by the amount of adverse excursion they showed. Using the data from Table 3.3, Table 3.4 sorts the winners and losers by the sizes of their MAEs. Table 3.5 shows the frequency of winners and losers in each bin.

7. *Graph the summary table.* Last, convert the summary table into a chart. If everything so far has been done in a spreadsheet, plotting won't be difficult.[6] Figure 3.3 shows our summary chart.

Figure 3.3 has some useful information for us already. Trading these rules in 1983–1984 would not have been too difficult with a $600 stop loss; we didn't see a single trade that exceeded that. If

---

[6] Unfortunately, MAE is not a technique that's taken fire since its publication in 1985. I'm not aware of publicly available software that explicitly does this, though there are trading systems and private software that use the idea. MetaStock for Windows does record the MAEs in its testing reports.

TABLE 3.4   **BINNING.** The MAEs of trades in Table 3.3
are dumped into different bins by their size.

MAE	0–.30	.31–.60	.61–.90	.91–1.20	1.21–1.50	1.51+
Winners	.07, .01, .08, 0, .06, 0, .04, .15, .07, .27					
Losers	.08, .02, .25	.46				

this were reliable (and it isn't, given the low number of trades), we'd
be comfortable using the $600 figure and also trading the market
with our $30,000. The chart would be solid evidence that our total
capital and loss amounts per trade were realistic.

Look, too, at the shape of the two curves. The winning curve
amounts to a single column but, if things truly were random, it
should have been smeared all over the different bins.

In a phenomenon we'll see repeated, the size of the adverse price
movements for winners is concentrated toward the left side of the
chart where the adverse excursion, measured in trading points, is
low or zero. Thus the rule that good trades just don't go far
against us.

TABLE 3.5   **SUMMARY TABLE.** The frequency of occurrences in each
bin is counted. Graph this table for convenience and analysis.

MAE	0–.30	.31–.60	.61–.90	.91–1.20	1.21–1.50	1.51+
Winners	10					
Losers	3	1				

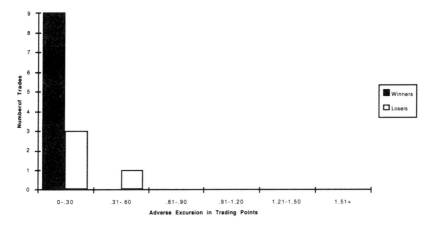

FIGURE 3.3   SUMMARY CHART. Number of trades versus adverse excursion, 1983–1984. Not only are there more winners (by happenstance) in this example, but they also tend to have low adverse price movement. This is only an illustrative chart as there aren't enough instances for the chart's information to be reliable or significant.

Meanwhile, the losing trades have a broader distribution of adverse excursion. Although there were only four of them in this example, one of them went 46 points in the hole before the trade tapped out. This phenomenon of large adverse excursions for losing trades is also common, perhaps necessarily.

To continue thinking about the shapes of these curves, what would it mean if the two distributions were shaped like those in Figure 3.4?

A chart without discernible, distinct patterns stems from trading rules that can't discern winners from losers. After all, winners just shouldn't go very far against you, whereas we expect losers to go the wrong way, yielding large adverse price movements. Being able to discern these distinct patterns is the first thing you want to achieve when looking at an MAE chart.

Last, Figure 3.3 gives a clue as to when to get out of a trade. The old adage "When you're wrong, get out!" gets an operational definition. You know you're wrong if your trade goes more than 30 ticks against you because, in this experience, winning trades just

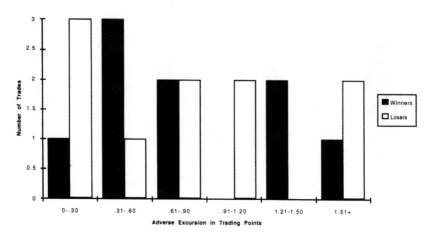

FIGURE 3.4   SMEARED. Number of trades versus adverse excursion during trade. Adverse price movement is spread randomly in this graph, indicating little difference between that of losing trades and that of winning trades. A display like this indicates that the trading rules have little ability to distinguish winners from losers.

don't go more than 30 ticks bad. You could even cut it more finely by breaking down the first bin (0 to .30) into, say, four bins (0 to .07, .08 to .15, .16 to .22, and .23 to .30). Table 3.6 shows the winners' and losers' MAEs broken down into these quarter-size bins, and Table 3.7 shows the frequency of winners and losers in each bin. Figure 3.5 presents these data in a chart that illustrates the winners' high concentration of low adverse excursion and the losers' greater spread.

Keeping mind that this is an exemplary chart, the question now should be "Exactly where would the stop go if we believed this

TABLE 3.6   TRADES BY BIN.

MAE	0–.07	.08–.15	.16–.22	.23–.30	.31–.37	.38–.45	.46–.52
Winners	.07, .01, 0, .06, .04, .07	.08, .15		0.27			
Losers	0.02	0.08		0.25			0.46

TABLE 3.7 FREQUENCY BY BIN.

MAE	0–.7	.8–.15	.16–.22	.23–.30	.31–.37	.38–.45	.46–.52
Winners	6	2		1			
Losers	1	1	1				1

chart?" Well, one place would be at 30 ticks (.30). The rule would be: Enter when both averages go upward or downward together and place a stop at 30 ticks opposite the direction of the trade. Table 3.8 shows the results.

What happened here was the reduction of a large loss. According to the rule of winning by minimizing the size of your largest loss, even this simple cutoff serves well. However, you might want to cut things even finer. Table 3.9 shows the effect of cutting off the trades at .08, or 8 ticks.

The effect of cutting off the trades at .08 is to reduce the net profit, but with lower loss potential since the largest loss would be just 8 ticks. You end up with 7 winners and 7 losers instead of 11 winners and 4 losers, showing the effect of setting stops too close. Don't believe for a moment you're going to trade Crude mechanically with an 8-tick stop, but the idea of being able to test the im-

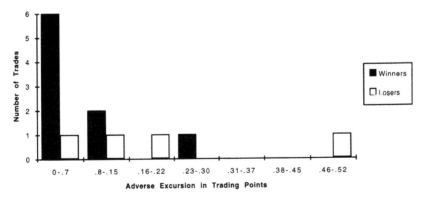

FIGURE 3.5 QUARTER-SIZE BINS. Number of trades versus adverse excursion. Splitting the categories along the X axis in half shows the winners' extreme concentration in the low adverse excursion realm and the losers' greater spread.

TABLE 3.8   IMPACT OF STOPS.

	Net Profit or Loss
Before using stop	$4.56 - .58 = 3.98$
Using stop at .30	$4.56 - .48^{7} = 4.08$

pact of adjusting your stop should strike a chord. *Here is a practical method of adjusting the stops to the combination of loss and profit level you think is appropriate.*

Typically, profit will decline as you accept less and less chance of loss, just as you'd expect. With enough trades, you could picture the tradeoff. Table 3.10 shows how this calculation would run, and Figure 3.6 presents these data as a chart.

Seen in graphic format, finding the cutoff point between loss and profit usually is feasible. By happenstance, this peculiar section of Crude data shows a sharp tradeoff with stops set at .08 and .15. After that, there's not much additional money to be made for absorbing adverse excursion beyond 15 ticks.

Results Using Crude Oil

An example is fine for learning, but what are the results of actually using this procedure on 3,069 days of perpetual Crude data? Figure 3.7 shows the actual results in the long term. Table 3.11 shows the frequency of winners and losers in each bin.

TABLE 3.9   CALCULATING STOP IMPACT.

	Net Profit or Loss
Before using stop	$4.56 - .58 = \mathbf{3.98}$
Using stop at .08	$.09 + .7 - .08 + .08 + .35 + .34 + .25 - .08$ $+ .05 - .08 - .08 - .08 - .08 - .02 = \mathbf{1.36}$

---

[7] $.48 = .58 - (.40 - .30)$. This reduces the size of the loss on the large loser from a net profit of .40 to .30.

TABLE 3.10 CALCULATING NET PROFITS.

Stop Level	0.08	0.15	0.22	0.3	0.37	0.45	0.52
Net Profit Computation	.09 + .7 −.08 + .08 +.35 + .34 +.25 − .08 +.05 − .08 −.08 − .08 −.08 − .02	0.09 + 0.7 + 0.08 + 0.35 +0.34 − 0.25 + 0.05 + 1.89 + 0.57 − (1 × 0.15) − 0.02 − 0.04 − 2 × 0.15	0.09 + 0.7 + 0.08 + 0.35 + 0.34 + 0.25 + 0.05 + 1.89 +0.57 − (1 × 0.22) − 0.02 − 0.04 − 2 × 0.22	0.09 + 0.7 + 0.08 + 0.35 + 0.34 + 0.25 + 0.05 + 1.89 + 0.57 + 0.24 − 0.02 − 0.04 −0.12 − 1 × 0.3	0.09 + 0.7 + 0.08+ 0.35 + 0.34 + 0.25 + 0.05 + 1.89 +0.57 + 0.24 − 0.02 − 0.04 −0.12 − 1 × 0.37	0.09 + 0.7 + 0.08 + 0.35 + 0.34 + 0.25 + 0.05 + 1.89 +0.57 + 0.24 − 0.02 − 0.04 −0.12 −1 × 0.45	0.09 + 0.7 + 0.08 + 0.35 + 0.34 + 0.25 + 0.05 + 1.89 + 0.57 + 0.24 − 0.02 − 0.04 − 0.12 − 0.4
Net Profit in Trading Points	1.36	3.81	3.60	4.08	4.01	3.93	3.98

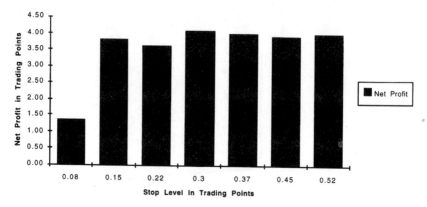

FIGURE 3.6   NET PROFIT VS. STOP LEVEL. A stop level of .15 seems to capture nearly all the profit available from this trading system, though higher profits are available at a stop level of .3. Gathering MAE information makes this analysis possible.

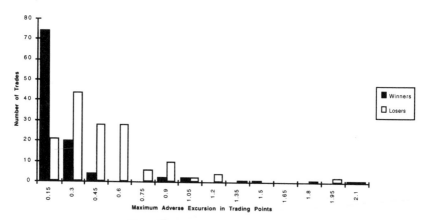

FIGURE 3.7   CRUDE MAE. Number of trades by maximum adverse excursion, 1983–1994, two-moving-average trading rule. Nearly all wins showed adverse price movement of no more than .3 or 30 ticks, whereas more than half the losers showed adverse movement of more than 30 ticks. The sharp distinction between the two distributions is the basis for implementing MAE stops.

(Perpetual data computed and delivered by CSI, Inc.)

TABLE 3.11   MAE DISTRIBUTION TRADING CRUDE OIL.
Bin size indicates a range, for example, .3 includes all trades
with adverse excursions ranging from .16 to .3.

MAE	0.15	0.3	0.45	0.6	0.75	0.9	1.05	1.2	1.35	1.5	1.65	1.8	1.95	2.1	Total
Winners	74	20	4	0	0	2	2	0	0	1	0	0	0	1	104
Losers	21	44	28	28	6	10	2	4	1	0	0	1	2	1	148

The overall message of the example—that winners just don't go very far against you—is borne out in this larger sample of data. Nearly all the winners are clustered in the first two bins, whereas the losers, despite a substantial 65 in the first two bins, also have more than half of their number in bins .45 and larger. This gives us the chance to make an operational distinction—placing stops—between winners and losers.

For example, what if we said we'll just stop out trades with an adverse excursion of more than 31 ticks or roughly $300? Clearly we'd cut off a lot of trades with larger MAEs but we'd also lose 10 trades (4 + 2 + 2 + 1 + 1) that were eventual winners even though they had large MAEs. What's the net effect? Figure 3.8 summarizes the effect of different stop levels in our exemplary Crude trading:

The Edge

This cutoff line beyond which winning trades rarely go may be the long-sought "edge" in trading. Knowing where the line is—knowing where to put one's stops based on actual experience—doesn't guarantee future success, but it's a lot more rational than arbitrary dollar figures (money management stops), percentage stops, indicator stops, or other nonexperiential stops. Because the cutoff line is quantifiable, it speeds up the process of implementing experience you'd otherwise gain over years of experimenting on stop placement. The funny thing, though, is that the edge has nothing to do with finding a good trade, only with minimizing the trade's losses.

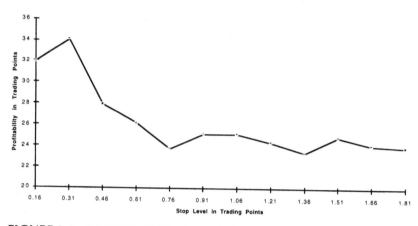

FIGURE 3.8   PROFITABILITY. Profitability versus size of stop, 1983–1995, two-moving-average trading rule. As the stop gets bigger, profits peak then decline steadily before going roughly flat. Traders using the information in Figure 3.7 would use this to choose between stops at .31 and .46.

The edge does something else for you: quite often, its use can convert a losing system to a winner or take a set of rules that loses more often than it wins and make it profitable. There's also a tremendous benefit from being protected from wipeout, a catastrophic loss. Perhaps with the experiential evidence gathered this way, you'll be sufficiently confident to use stops or something operationally equivalent. Just using MAE stops should materially improve your trading.

THE ARGUMENT FROM EXPERIENCE

Stop for a moment and think about what's been done here.

We've tabulated the actual experience resulting from following an explicit set of entry and exit rules. They could have been any rules; the analysis of adverse price movement would not have changed. What expectation is there that the experience will carry forward into the future? Certainly, the markets that trade in the future will not experience the same shocks that markets in the past have experienced. The result will be adverse excursions outside what we expect, and I will take different small losses than I expect. That's fine as long as they're small, though. If adverse price movement is less than I've experienced in the past, all the better.

Admittedly, letting experience set stop levels is not complicated, but the very simplicity gives it durability.

The charts of adverse movement also give an immediate picture of whether a set of trading rules can distinguish between good trades (i.e., ones that don't go far bad) and bad trades. If the rules don't generate distinctly different distributions, they are likely to be meaningless. They immediately answer the question "What happens when I trade a specific market in a specific way?"

What I really like about this sort of analysis of experience is that it's imperceptible to competitive traders and analysts bound up in parametric statistics and charts. Moreover, because it's applicable to any set of trading rules, its results are unique and my stops are less likely to rest around the levels where everyone else normally clusters.

EXEMPLARY TRADING

The chapters ahead use this technique within the context of a campaign of trading. Although there are far too many data to show all 252 trades from trending alone, I do want you to have some sense for how this underlying trend system trades so that when we talk about refinements later, you'll have a head start. As a trending system, it's usually late and subject to whipsaws. Its good points are that it never misses a trend and rarely countertrades into a trend. Figures 3.9 and 3.10 show the good side and the ugly side of our trend trader.

Although you haven't gone through all 3,069 days yourself, you can see from these charts that the normal amounts of misery and elation are to be had from this system. It will prove to be normally cantankerous in trying to make money as we add refinements to this basic approach.

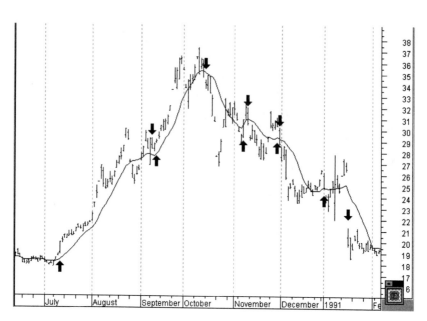

FIGURE 3.9 THE GOOD. Like a good trending system, our two-moving-average example reliably catches every trend, though things rarely go this smoothly in the real world.

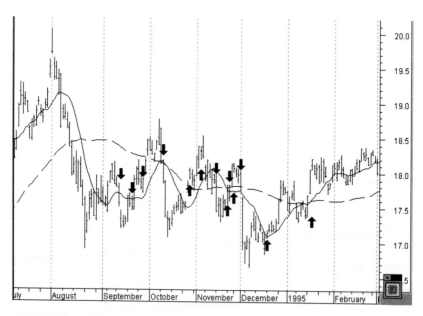

FIGURE 3.10 THE UGLY. Our underlying system trades just as experience would indicate during whipsaw trading: badly.

CAMPAIGN WRAP-UP

Just as in a war there will be casualties, so in campaigning there will be losses. The campaigning trader, having studied the ground, will have a pretty good idea of the size and frequency of those losses (and the wins) from his or her study of adverse price movement from the point of entry.

Before going on to use this technique on live data, you should feel pretty comfortable that you understand how MAE is calculated and why you'd use it. Using this concept, the next chapter will step directly into testing different vehicles.

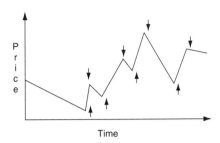

4
Testing

In this chapter, we pick what contracts to test and subsequently trade. For stocks there is no choice, but futures offer a variety of contracts we may use. Using New York Light Crude as an example, we look at the testing from the standpoint of loss control and profitability before selecting a testing vehicle for our campaign.

Testing trading systems has been covered thoroughly in other publications[1] so I'll hit only the highlights here, particularly with respect to crude oil.

Testing in general is suspect because we aren't dealing with a repetitive process where we expect to find x that causes y. We are painfully aware that the world is evolving and changing. Therefore, the markets are evolving and changing. New markets come into being and old markets fade away; new stocks are created and old favorites die, dissolve, or fall out of favor. The ground on which we validate our trading rules won't be the ground on which they are used.

---

[1] Tushar S. Chande and Stanley Kroll, *The New Technical Trader* (New York: John Wiley and Sons, Inc., 1994). Charles Le Beau and David W. Lucas, *Technical Traders Guide to Computer Analysis of the Futures Market* (Homewood: Irwin, 1992). Bruce Babcock, Jr., *The Business One Irwin Guide to Trading Systems* (Homewood: Business One, 1989).

What may be consistent—and we have weak evidence of this—is crowd behavior. Many speculative bubbles have been documented historically, and these occur even in laboratory situations.[2] It may be that the behavior of crowds in times of stress is consistent. Personally, I believe that fear and greed (mostly fear), despair and hope, drive most adult actions. People in a fearful state are not calculating probabilistic, discounted, future cash flows! However, in large numbers, their actions may be consistent. That is my assumption, at any rate.

There is other evidence. Just in terms of national and international economics, it's tough after experiencing two or three business cycles to ignore the feeling that comes over you that some events are relatively predictable. Cyclical content in economic time series has been analyzed for several centuries and the "business cycle" is a workaday business concept. I recall, for example, the asset/liability management committee of a bank where I worked being quite comfortable with its interest rate outlook, the Fed's stance, and its consequent positioning of the bank's balance sheet to exploit the business cycle.

In the end, the rationale for testing, whether on paper or with AudiTrack,[3] is that there is no alternative preparation for putting money at risk in technical speculation. So we might as well get on with it.

YOUR PERSONAL EXPERIENCE

One thing that can be said in testing's favor is that it accelerates the building of our own experience with the market. There is certainly

---

[2] Ronald R. King, Vernon L. Smith, Arlington W. Williams, and Mark Van Boening, "The Robustness of Bubbles and Crashes in Experimental Stock Markets," in R. Day and P. Chen, *Non-linear Dynamics and Evolutionary Economics* (Oxford: Oxford Press, 1993), pp. 182–200. Vernon Smith at the Economic Science Laboratory, University of Arizona, is an excellent resource on this topic.

[3] AudiTrack is a real-time paper broker to whom orders can be phoned for accounting and tabulation of trading records. AUDITRACK, Inc., (407) 393-3876.

craft in trading. We just don't know what it is, precisely; how to formalize it; or how to hand it on. Institutionally, it's usually learned on the job with more or less supervision and guidance depending on the house.

For individual traders, there's learning by observing for several years, but few follow that path. The other way is stepping through trades day by day, by hand, with charts. I recommend this ancient practice because you have many chances to both fool yourself and be honest with yourself. The distinction will eventually dawn on you. You learn quite viscerally the difficulties of trading in the manner you propose and you pick up the patterns that make sense to you. Creating charts is much better for learning patterns than simply reviewing a raft of them on a screen or shuffling through 200 printouts from a screening program. These somehow fail to build an impression in one's mind, whereas manually plotting charts day after day does inculcate one, perhaps through some subconscious process, with usable intuition.

When it comes to testing, the alternative to personal experience is reading the nifty trading summaries produced by computers and their software. While these outputs are objective, I suggest that the only interesting things on these summaries are the net profits line and the risk measures such as the Sharp Ratio or Traynor Index. I'm in the minority here, most people look at the percentage of successful trades, number of winning or losing longs or shorts, and so forth. These items are secondary. We know going in that if you control the size of your losses, you can later worry about being right more often.

SCIENTIFIC PROCESS

The first step in a scientific process is direct observation and measurement. Shortly, I'll show you more of this than you'll want to see, but it's important to know where we're at regarding market phenomena. At this stage of market knowledge, simply identifying and measuring distinct phenomena in market behavior is a step forward. There may be private practitioners who've gone farther in the scientific process and developed theory, but my sense of the situation is that we are at stage one and no proper theory of market behavior exists. I'm not proposing one, nor do I say that I'm undertaking even the observational process properly. I'm a trader, not an investigator. I only hope to place my observations in their proper frame of reference, leave a thorough investigation to others, and exploit their use now for my own gain.

Therefore, when we do undertake testing of a trading system, we do so with a grain of salt. Prudence forces us to estimate our chances of success, and we have no other means than looking at historical performance, knowing full well that the future campaign will not be the same as the last one. Our hope is that the reactions of the market's mob will be of the type, speed, and nature of its reactions in the past. Occasionally (1987, for example)[4] this is not true, but day in and day out, we cannot perceive great differences in behavior, so we defer to necessity and test.

IN SAMPLE OR OUT OF SAMPLE

It's thought that, ideally, when testing a trading system, we'd create it using one set of data and test it on a second, third, or fourth set, perhaps stepping forward in time as we do so. This might give us an opportunity to discover problems with the trading rules and modify the rules somewhat, always keeping in mind that the more elaborate the rules, the more rigid the system[5] and the less likely it is to behave robustly in the future. Actually, all stepping forward does is increase the responsiveness of our rules if we continually modify them. It cannot change the fact that we are testing on the

---

[4] My verdict on 1987 is that too many people were trying to get through the door at the same time. The market's physical incapacity to handle the volume and financial incapacity to handle the direction exacerbated the downward movement on virtually no shift in the fundamentals.

[5] See the many discussions in trading literature of overfitting and statistical degrees of freedom. For simplicity and directness, see Bob Pelletier, "An Official Guide to Trading System Design," CSI Technical Journal, vol. X, numbers 9, 10, and 11.

past for a very different future. Our only true defense is keeping the rules simple.

This is contrary to the instinct of the novice developer who thinks that by piling on more rules, more ifs, and more filters, the system becomes more refined and specific. As it turns out, we'd generally like to get by with one, two, or at most three decision rules; our knowledge of market behavior is that vague. This general guidance is one reason moving averages are useful: they are simple.

Another point: When testing, you'd like to get enough samples to accurately portray the underlying rules of the entire population of trades (assuming the rules aren't changing). The more rules, the more samples you'll need to have confidence that your sample does replicate things. Because the rule of thumb is to get at least 30 of what you're after, the typical trading system that has 1 winner for every 2 losers may need 90 trades (30 winners and 60 losers) to be safely in the ballpark. Thus there is a demand for lots of data to use in testing.

DETAILS OF SPECIFIC CONTRACTS

The first difficulty in testing is determining what to test because different trading vehicles have different tradable horizons. A stock, for example, is obviously traded year-round. Developing rules on 1983 data and testing them on 1996 data works out easily.

In contrast, the most tradable bond changes with the shape of the yield curve, pricing differentials, and supply, among many factors. It's been impossible for me to find a consistent time series of bond pricing with realistic daily ranges for individual issues, even governments, making testing cash bond trading systems more of a problem than I could handle.

Futures contracts are exchange-traded but are more complicated than stocks, having various delivery months and definite deliveries that are "most active." Not only does developing something on an active month and testing it on an inactive month not work well (because daily ranges are different), but there may not be enough data in the off month to even test. Each contract is also peculiar to its commercial market and its seasonality, with the exception of the financials, though people sporadically publish evidence of seasonality here, too.[6]

One solution to facilitate testing has been continuous contracts, artificial time series that are cobbled together from the underlying real contracts. Another solution is to step through the actual rollover process that you'll follow in real life, thereby generating realistic amounts of slippage[7] and commissions. A third solution is to find a contract or possibly two that are adequately active year-round and roll once or twice a year. I prefer the third alternative but use the first and occasionally fight through the second depending on the item being traded.

Of the continuous contracting methods, I use the perpetual contract created by CSI.[8] This is a rolling, 90-day, weighted average of the front two contracts' prices. It generates a time series that has a consistent, realistic daily range, a factor that is vital in analyzing adverse price movement, at least initially. It is also statistically stationary.[9] Once I've analyzed the contracts using perpetual data, I jump to the contract that trades well year-round, if it exists, on failing that, to the most active contracts in the commodity or financial tradable. There, I repeat the analysis to see if the stop levels change materially.[10] My adjustments, if any, are usually on the order of a tick or three. Probably the most tedious example of this process possible is the contract for New York Light Crude.

---

[6] For examples, see *Moore Research Center Report*, various issues, Moore Research Center, Inc., 321 West 13th Avenue, Eugene, OR 97401. Phone (503) 484-7256, FAX (503) 484-2202.

[7] Slippage is the difference between the estimated or ordered transaction price and the actual price received on the order.

[8] Commodity Systems, Inc., Boca Raton, FL. Phone (407) 392-8663. Today most people ask for CSI's Code 46 contract instead of the original Code 39 contract. Code 46 does best on contracts that trade frequently, like Crude.

[9] A stationary time series is one in which the underlying rules that generate the time series do not change over time. See Clifford J. Sherry, *The Mathematics of Technical Analysis* (Chicago: Probus, 1992), p. 9.

[10] It's a refinement beyond the scope of this book to analyze the change in the range as the contract draws nearer to expiration. The closer to expiration, the wider the range, and a sophisticated analyst may adjust MAE stops accordingly.

DETAILS OF NEW YORK LIGHT CRUDE

Crude contracts are most liquid for about two nearby months, but the December and June contracts are liquid several years into the future. That is to say, for example, they have solid open interest in the December 1998 contract during June of 1995 even if trading volume is much lighter in the out months. This can be seen in Figure 4.1, where the 1998 contracts show very little range while at the same time the 1995 contracts are quite dynamic.

Another difficulty in selecting the right contract to analyze is that daily range typically widens as the contracts near expiration. If you simply looked at correlations between perpetual contract values and actual contract values, you'd find them running in the .9 range, close to the perfect 1.0. However, practical trading is more

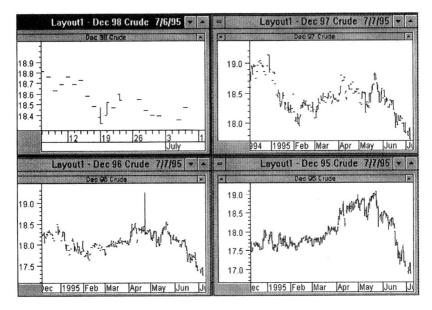

FIGURE 4.1   DECEMBER CRUDE. Nearby and distant Crude contracts. Daily range drops dramatically in the distant Crude oil contracts despite a substantial open interest. The Crude contracts are prime hedging vehicles, but the nearby two or three contracts are best for daily trading.
Data source: Dial Data, Inc.

difficult. As the previous contract expires, volume floods into the next active contract, resulting in more excesses of pricing and wider ranges. This can be seen in the daily range of the June 1995 New York Light Crude contract shown in Figure 4.2.

In contrast, the perpetual contract flattens out this surge in the last two months, as shown in Figure 4.3.

This phenomenon happens to some extent in all commodities, necessitating some consideration when testing for stop levels using adverse price movements. (In stocks, there are certainly volume and range surges but not, in my small experience, seasonally.) The convenience of using a perpetual contract runs into the practicality of trading the real thing. You don't want to develop a test during the quiet periods and test it or trade it later on an active period—you're going to find a lot of those closely set stops hit. There's no substitute for examining the behavior of each trading vehicle, so instead of using the perpetual for testing and trading signals, we'll check some actual contracts. (Again, this digression deals only with futures, not with stocks, so your technique needs to be specific to

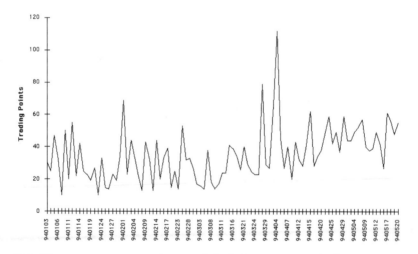

FIGURE 4.2   DAILY RANGE. Crude's daily range, June 1995. In a typical phenomenon, June 1994 New York Light Crude daily range expands as the contract nears expiration. The widening range has a direct impact on adverse price movement estimates.

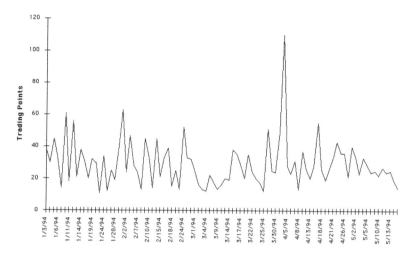

FIGURE 4.3   PERPETUAL RANGES. Daily ranges in perpetual Crude. In contrast to the June 1995 Crude daily ranges, the perpetual contract does not show the shift upward in the last months of trading of the June contract. Traders testing for MAE stops need to adjust for this phenomenon.

the futures market you're trading.) Generally, finish testing with data you'd actually trade.

Crude is a good example because it's a highly liquid market with certain contracts that are more active than others plus a definite seasonality. Moreover, it trades in a complex of petroleum-related contracts that are constantly arbitraged among each other and against cash or physicals,[11] thereby influencing each other by their individual supply and demand. These considerations—time to expiration, seasonality, popularity, and arbitrage—affect the volume in a contract at different times.

A New York Light Crude contract trading on the New York Mercantile Exchange expires every month of the year, so you could trade something expiring in any month. However, the December Crude contract is the most popular, the bellwether, showing the

---

[11] Physicals is a term that refers to the delivery of the actual commodity, in this case crude oil.

highest open interest the furthest in the future. Next most popular is the June contract, following the same considerations. Correlations between June and December are in the .9 range, as are correlations between these two contracts and the other monthly contracts.

To avoid testing and trading every single month serially during trend trading, you could trade December only or June and December and find your overall trend signals fitting very well with trading the nearby and rolling constantly. Practically, this would also minimize commissions and slippage on rollovers.

However, the techniques in Chapter 3 are very sensitive to highs and lows. The question is whether the appropriate MAE stops would change over the year if the daily ranges expanded as you got closer to expiration. To answer this, you'd look first at the daily range experience. Figure 4.4 shows examples of 4 of the 11 December Crude contracts available for analysis in 1995.

Just from these four graphs, you can see that daily range is *very* dynamic. Would it be a good idea to adjust MAE stops by daily range as the contract neared expiration? Perhaps, but the process is intricate so I leave it for a more technical examination elsewhere. For the purposes of campaigning, we need only be aware of this refinement.

For testing purposes, I first tested using the monthly contracts (for example, trading June during the month of April, then trading July in May, and so on). Then I tested using each year's December contract from November of the previous year through the end of October.[12] To both the monthly continuous and the December contract, I applied the trading rules and checked the MAE charts. I checked to see whether to use a yearly contract or the month to month alternative. Occasionally, these different views are nearly identical, but in a contract as active as Crude, it's not likely, thereby increasing your workload as you select the approach most useful for actual trading.

---

[12] When rolling from one month to another, I calculate my stops in the new contract by using the new contract's price point on the day the trade was entered. For example, on January 15 you go long at the close of $20 in the March contract. April is at $20.50 on the same day. Your stop is 45 points away at $20–.45 = $19.55. The equivalent stop in April will be $20.50–.45 = $20.05.

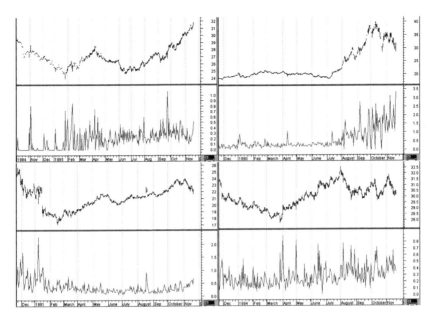

FIGURE 4.4   VOLATILITY IN THE DECEMBER CONTRACT. Daily ranges in the December New York Light Crude contract fluctuate with the season, activity in the market, nearness to expiration, wars—you name it. Because MAE stops are sensitive to daily range, you must analyze this carefully to select the best contracts to both test and trade. Stock traders should see less seasonality.

To spare you the agony of detail this entails, I've summarized the results graphically for each year in Figure 4.5. Note in each pairing that the chart on the top shows the number of winning trades and the number of losing trades by the maximum adverse price movement the trades experienced en route to closure. You should note where the bulk of the winning trades lie, as well as the bulk of the losing trades. There should be a distinct difference, or else our trading system cannot distinguish good from bad.

Below the MAE chart is the chart of profitability as the stop is widened by the size of the bins used for classification. In nearly every case, you'll see discernible peaks. Because it's difficult for the eye to see patterns between charts, Figures 4.6 and 4.7 show the

(text continues on page 88)

FIGURE 4.5 MONTHLY CONTRACTS WITH ROLLOVER, 1984–1994.

These graphs for 1984–1994 were created from monthly contracts with rollover on the last day of the most active trading month. Commissions and slippage are not included. You can compare these to the graphs produced by the December contracts in Figure 4.8.

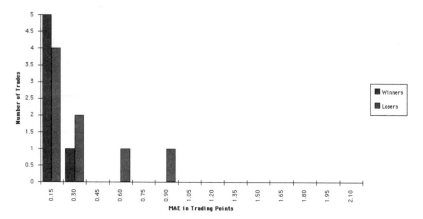

1984. Winning and losing trades versus MAE. This graph shows that there were five winning trades with a maximum adverse excursion of .15 or less and four winning trades with the same performance.

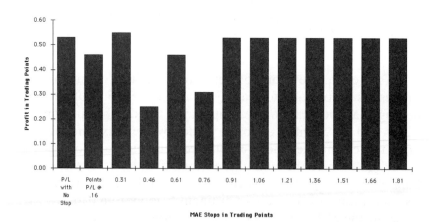

1984. Profitability versus MAE stop. Look at this graph to check profitability. The first bar shows profits with no stops. The second bar shows profits with the first MAE stop, in this case .16 or 16 trading points.

FIGURE 4.5   (*Continued*)

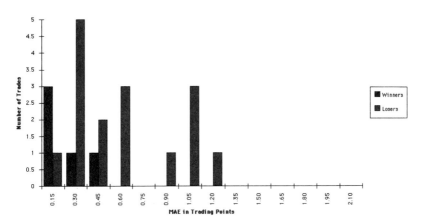

1985. Winning and losing trades versus MAE. This chart shows a clear distinction between the adverse movement of winners and that of losers.

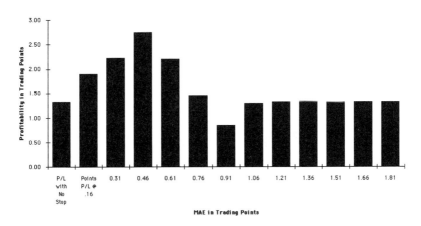

1985. Profitability versus MAE stop. Here, as the winners are added in by widening stops, they manage to overcome the increasing number of losers that aren't cut short. This is not always what happens.

FIGURE 4.5   MONTHLY CONTRACTS WITH ROLLOVER, 1984–1994.
(*Continued*)

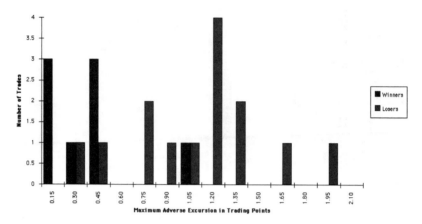

1986. Winning and losing trades versus MAE.

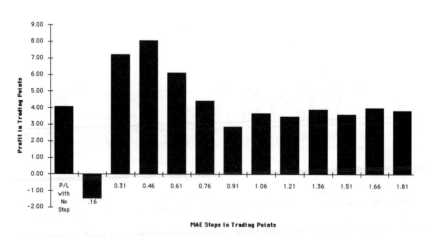

1986. Profitability versus MAE stop.

FIGURE 4.5 (*Continued*)

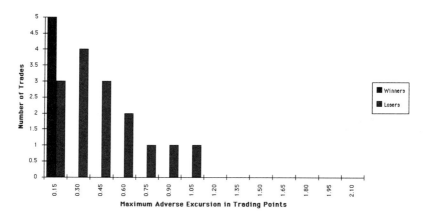

1987. Winning and losing trades versus MAE.

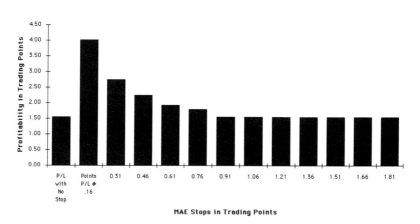

1987. Profitability versus MAE stop.

FIGURE 4.5   MONTHLY CONTRACTS WITH ROLLOVER, 1984–1994. (*Continued*)

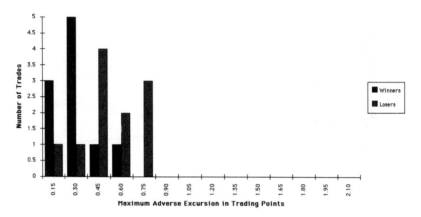

1988. Winning and losing trades versus MAE.

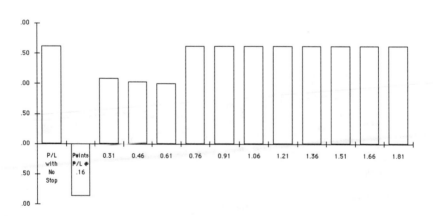

1988. Profitability versus MAE stop.

FIGURE 4.5 (*Continued*)

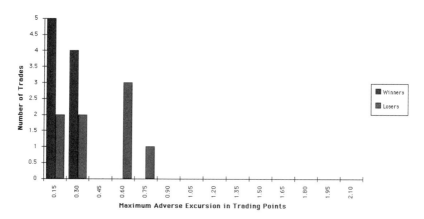

1989. Winning and losing trades versus MAE.

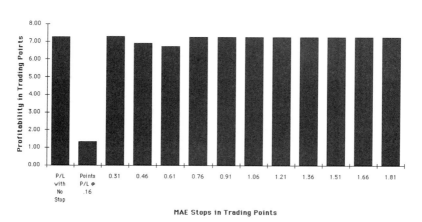

1989. Profitability versus MAE stop.

**FIGURE 4.5   MONTHLY CONTRACTS WITH ROLLOVER, 1984–1994.
(*Continued*)**

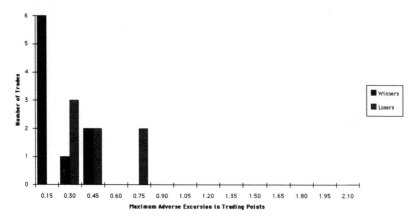

1990. Winning and losing trades versus MAE.

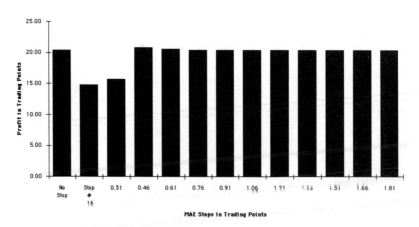

1990. Profitability versus MAE stop.

FIGURE 4.5   (*Continued*)

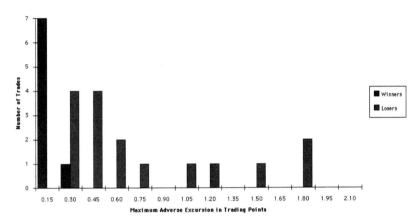

1991. Winning and losing trades versus MAE. This is a sobering twosome. You can have all your winners clustered with MAE under .16 and still barely come out ahead. In 1991, this system's winners were tiny and its losers huge.

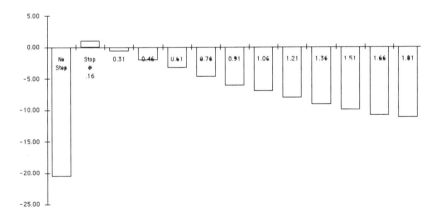

1991. Profitability versus MAE stop.

FIGURE 4.5   MONTHLY CONTRACTS WITH ROLLOVER, 1984–1994. (*Continued*)

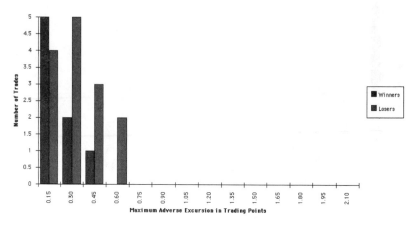

1992. Winning and losing trades versus MAE.

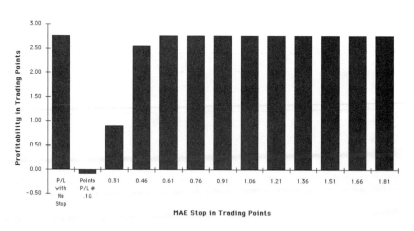

1992. Profitability versus MAE stop.

FIGURE 4.5   (*Continued*)

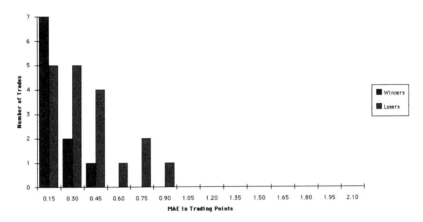

1993. Winning and losing trades versus MAE.

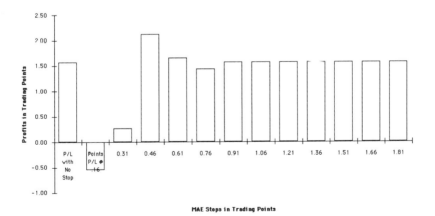

1993. Profitability versus MAE stop.

FIGURE 4.5   MONTHLY CONTRACTS WITH ROLLOVER, 1984–1994. (*Continued*)

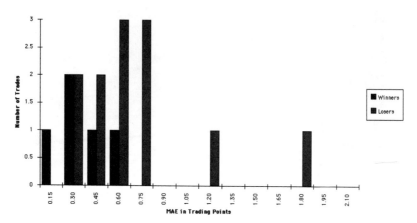

1994. Winning and losing trades versus MAE.

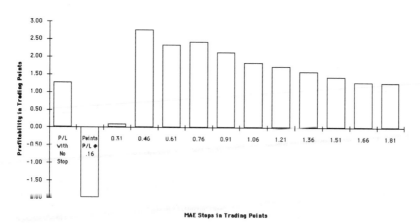

1994. Profitability versus MAE stop.

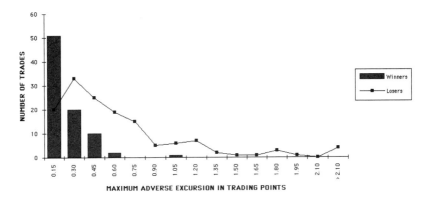

FIGURE 4.6   MONTHLY CRUDE MAE. Winners and losers versus MAE, 1984–1994. Using each monthly contract as it comes up shows the usual distribution of winners with MAE less than .15 and losers with MAE peaking at .3 then tailing off to the right. Compare this figure to Figure 3.11 in Chapter 3 and to Figure 4.9.

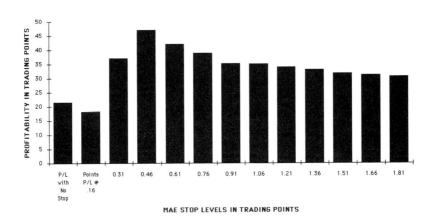

FIGURE 4.7   MONTHLY PROFITABILITY. Profitability versus MAE, 1984–1994. Showing a smooth rise in profitability as stops are increased to .46, trading all 12 monthly contracts consecutively comes closest to an intuitive result.

results summarized for all ten years. The summary charts are comparable to the charts for the perpetual contract in Chapter 3.[13]

Before going on to the graphs produced using just the December contracts, a few observations:

1. I see relative stability about the stop point at .46, which is the fourth bin from the left. Setting a stop at .46 for a trend trade didn't always produce the most profit, but it was always close and at $460 per contract it's pretty reasonable. Generally, .46 was in hindsight either the best choice for the year or the next best choice. For slightly lower losses, stops at .31 still generated a good profit.

2. You can "step forward" yourself with this graph series by, for example, picking a stop level from the 1984 chart and seeing how it would work in 1985. Repeat the process for succeeding years.

3. Generally, setting stops closer than .46 was tougher on profits. This confirms experience that stops set too closely are simply likely to be picked off, probably by normally noisy market action. It may be that Crude's noise level in the nearby contract is somewhere below 46 trading points.

4. The general ratio of wins to losses here is about 1:2, a depressing but realistic number in the trading systems development world. This exemplary averages system gives maximum adverse excursion a lot of damage to limit.

In conclusion: Based on experience, you could definitely both trade and test on the monthly contracts. You'd find it tedious but workable. The next question is whether life couldn't be simpler by using, for example, the December contract.

---

[13] The year of trading shown here is the January through December contracts for each year. They were tested from November of the previous year through October of the nominal year.

Using the December Contract

An alternative to trading month to month is to trade the most active contract of the year, perhaps adjusting for the increasing volatility over the year. I find this works well for the large active markets. Each trader will make a judgment on this, but for now all we need is a tool to make the choice. The question for Crude is "Which to use, monthly or yearly?" Let's see if there's much difference. Figure 4.8 shows MAE and profitability of New York Light Crude December contracts for each year between 1984 and 1994. Figure 4.9 summarizes MAE for 1984–1994 December contracts, and Figure 4.10 summarizes profitability for 1984–1994 December contracts.

Picking a Trading Series

Comparing Figures 3.7, 4.6, and 4.9, we see some remarkable consistencies (see Table 4.1), despite quite a bit of variation in individual years' results.

You don't need skew statistics to see that the distributions in Figure 4.9 are centered differently and lean differently—which simply means that winning trades perform differently from losing trades as far as adverse price movement goes. This confirms trading experience that good trades hardly go against you, and here we see how far they don't go against you—maybe 45 to 46 ticks.

One more thing before making a choice for campaigning: Look also at profitability, which is a more complicated picture. The profitability charts show the level of gain or loss from the trading rules given only one thing changing: the stops.

Say you decided to trade only the monthly contracts and with *no stops*. Experience from 1984 to 1994 shows you'd have seen ups and downs leading to a profit of 2,000 ticks over ten years. But what ups and downs you experienced. There'd have been 1987 with four trades having adverse price movement of up to 120 ticks. There'd have been 1991 where you'd have stepped into a hole 2,000 ticks deep in one year. You need to stop these killer events.

(text continues on page 102)

FIGURE 4.8   MAE AND PROFITABILITY DECEMBER CONTRACTS.

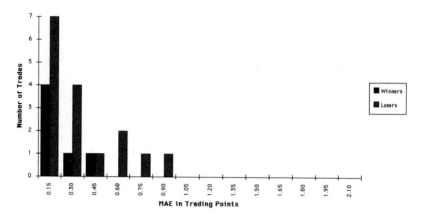

December 1984. Winning and losing trades versus MAE. This is about as bad as it gets. Here there are actually more losers clustered in the first bin than winners. The distinction between the two distributions is still clear.

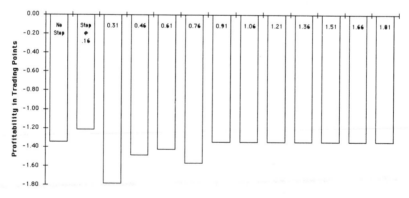

December 1984. Profitability versus MAE stop. Even tight stops couldn't save this year, but see below for the exact opposite: stops getting in the way.

FIGURE 4.8 (*Continued*)

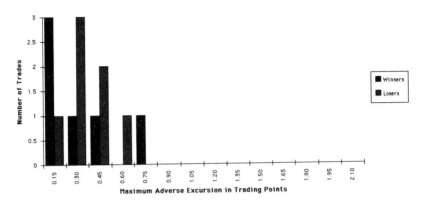

December 1985. Winning and losing trades versus MAE.

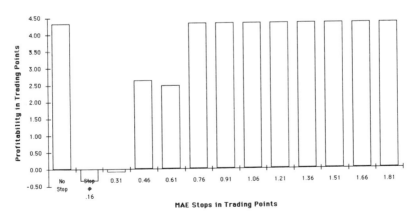

December 1985. Profitability versus MAE stop.

FIGURE 4.8   MAE AND PROFITABILITY DECEMBER CONTRACTS. (*Continued*)

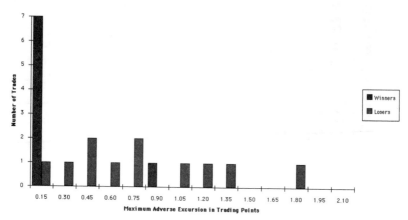

December 1986. Winning and losing trades versus MAE.

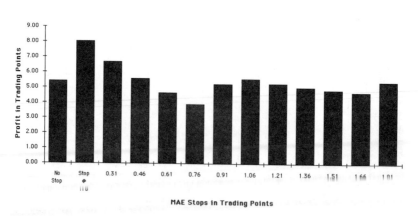

December 1986. Profitability versus MAE stop.

FIGURE 4.8   (*Continued*)

1987. Here's a depressing pair of graphs. You get excellent definition between the adverse movement of winners versus that of losers and you still can't pick a stop point. If you pick .16, you barely make money. Any greater and you lose. The wins just aren't big enough to cover the plethora of losers.

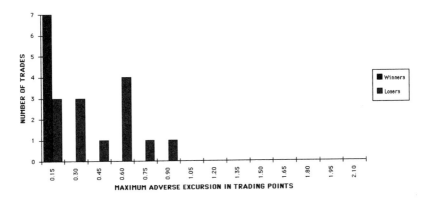

December 1987. Winning and losing trades versus MAE.

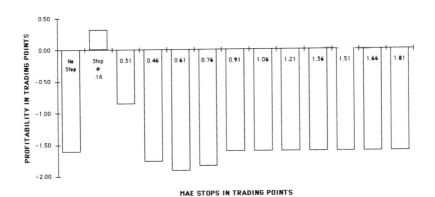

December 1987. Profitability versus MAE stop.

FIGURE 4.8   MAE AND PROFITABILITY DECEMBER CONTRACTS. (*Continued*)

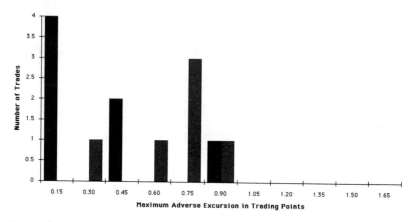

December 1988. Winning and losing trades versus MAE.

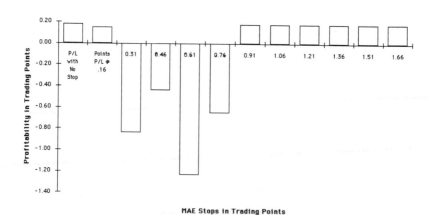

December 1988. Profitability versus MAE stop.

FIGURE 4.8 (*Continued*)

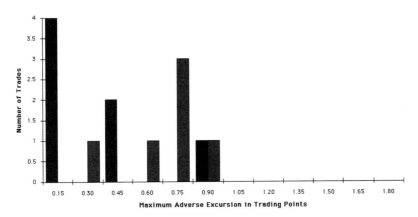

December 1989. Winning and losing trades versus MAE.

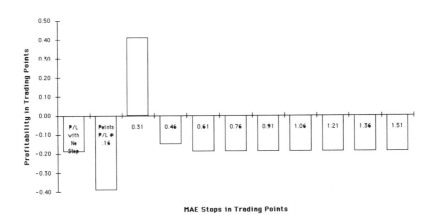

December 1989. Profitability versus MAE stop.

FIGURE 4.8   MAE AND PROFITABILITY DECEMBER CONTRACTS.
(*Continued*)

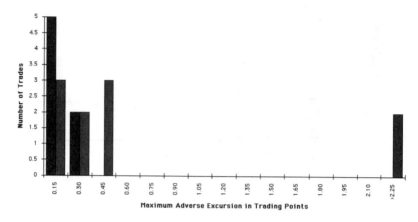

December 1990. Winning and losing trades versus MAE.

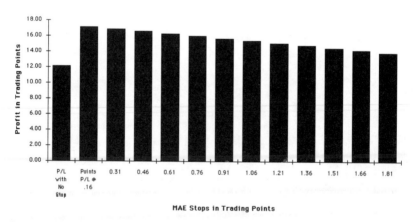

December 1990. Profitability versus MAE stop.

FIGURE 4.8 (*Continued*)

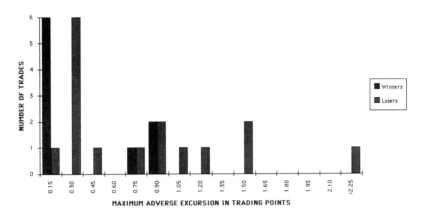

December 1991. Winning and losing trades versus MAE.

December 1991. Profitability versus MAE stop.

FIGURE 4.8   MAE AND PROFITABILITY DECEMBER CONTRACTS. (*Continued*)

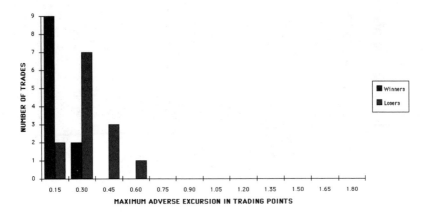

December 1992. Winning and losing trades versus MAE.

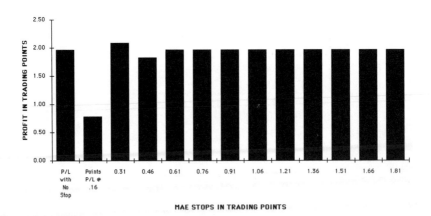

December 1992. Profitability versus MAE stop.

FIGURE 4.8   (*Continued*)

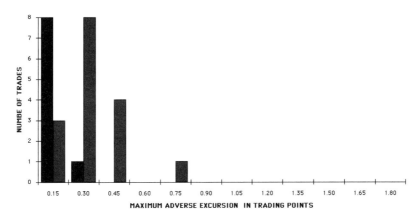

December 1993. Winning and losing trades versus MAE.

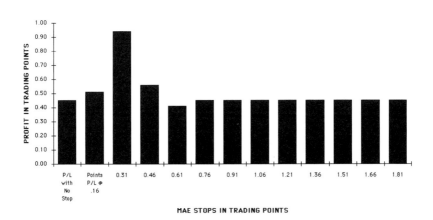

December 1993. Profitability versus MAE stop.

FIGURE 4.8   MAE AND PROFITABILITY DECEMBER CONTRACTS.
(*Continued*)

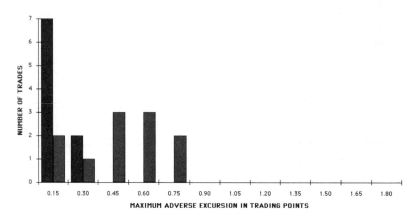

December 1994. Winning and losing trades versus MAE.

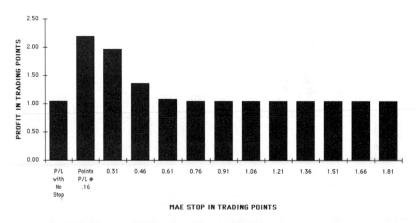

December 1994. Profitability versus MAE stop.

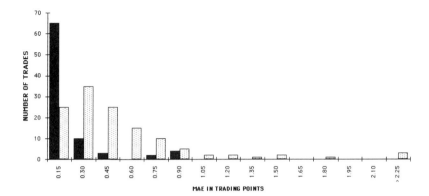

FIGURE 4.9   DECEMBER CRUDE MAE, 1984–1994. Winners and losers versus MAE. Trading just the December contract from November through October gives the usual peak of winners with very low MAE and a few winners with MAE as high as .9. Compare this figure to Figure 3.11 and Figure 4.6.

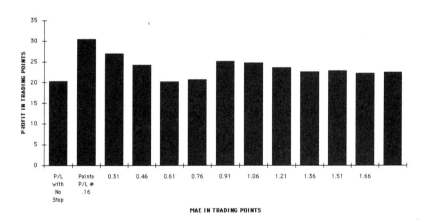

FIGURE 4.10   PROFITABILITY VS. MAE USING DECEMBER CONTRACTS 1984–1994. In contrast to Figure 4.7, trading just the December contracts shows quite varied results and a generally lower overall profit level. The peak at an MAE stop of only 16 ticks may reflect the quiet trading in the early months of the contract when ranges aren't nearly those of the active contract.

TABLE 4.1   COMPARING ANALYTICAL CONTRACTS.

Perpetual Contract	Monthly Contracts	December Contracts
Winning MAE peaks below a stop of .15	Winning MAE peaks below a stop of .15	Winning MAE peaks below a stop of .15
Losing MAE peaks between .16 and .30	Losing MAE peaks between .16 and .30	Losing MAE peaks between .16 and .30
Largest MAE for a winner is 2.1	Largest MAE for a winner is 1.05	Largest MAE for a winner is .9
Largest MAE for a loser is 2.1	Largest MAE for a loser is over 2.1	Largest MAE for a loser is over 2.25

Because the only operational tool at hand is a stop, what could that have done for you? A tight 16-tick stop trading Crude would have been trouble. It lowers your overall profitability but *it keeps you in the game.* If dropping ten years' profit in one year (about two-thirds of original capital in this example) would knock you out, even this too-tight stop would serve.

Going to a stop at .31 is better—it nearly doubles overall profitability while still keeping you in the game. Going to .46 bumps things up another 30% and still keeps you in the game. I stress this to remind you that we can't win if we can't play. We can't play if we *ever* lose big. The problem in the past has been finding stops that aren't too close and aren't too far. Now we have a tool for placing stops experientially.

Looking at the yearly profitability charts, I see all the action on the charts in the first four columns. Sometimes (e.g., 1989 and 1990), there doesn't seem to be much difference where your stop would be, but in most years, trading these rules, the most change in profitability comes from stop levels below .46. I speculated earlier that, given our trending trading rules, the noise level in Crude probably oscillates below .46. Most tradables have some noise band like this.

Bottom Line

By inspecting the experience with different trading vehicles (perpetual, monthly, or December contracts), I'd opt to trade the monthlies. Most traders would want to be in the most active contract to get the fastest fills with the lowest slippage. Although the MAE distributions are similar for all three approaches, using the monthly contracts gives the smoothest distributions, suggesting more underlying consistency. To cap it off, it's simply 30% more profitable to trade the monthlies, and either the .31 or the .46 MAE stop is well within the 2% of capital guideline. I'd choose the .31 level because at that level I have the choice of trading two contracts instead of one while staying under my $600 loss limit.

Our campaign of trading is off with a profitable set of underlying trading rules and a loss level lower than the limit of $600 per trade, as shown in Table 4.2.

SUMMARY

Is it worth it to know where, given our trading rules, our stop should be? The answer is definitely yes. We shouldn't trade without it.

Is it worth it to know what trading vehicle (contract) to use for analysis and engagement? You bet: sooner or later we must take off and we'd better be on the right flight when we go.

Is it a lot of work to determine which contract to use? Yes.

This chapter has shown what homework is necessary when using maximum adverse excursion by testing for the best stop level using perpetual, monthly, and December contracts for trading. We found the system could be profitable overall despite a low win–loss ratio and it could be more profitable with effectively placed stops when trading the most active month of the Crude contract.

TABLE 4.2   CAMPAIGN TRADING PROFITABILITY NEW YORK LIGHT CRUDE, 1984–1994.

Mode	Rule	Stop Level	Profit/Loss
Trend	Two moving averages	.31	3,600

5

Piling On: Exploiting the Trend

After the initial probe and entry, the main campaign gets under way. Although the battle ebbs and flows, if we find the enemy retreating we double our efforts. So it goes in trading: as the trades move along our line of advance, we look for places to commit additional resources.

Are we mindful that at some point the advance must end? Of course! At some point we will add another position to our trending trade and find out that the trend is no longer with us. Should we try to avoid this? No! Unless you are so prescient as to pick all tops and bottoms, you are going to take a loss at the end of a trend. What's more, your trending campaign will be filled with little losses, some more significant than others. It's up to you as the general to understand what stage you are in, but here I suggest some techniques for managing the campaign as you participate in a trend.

SITUATION

Assuming the initial trade wasn't stopped out promptly, we're in a trend mode with an underlying position long or short. Just *being* in a trend trade is the first indication of the trend. Many of these trades (about two-thirds of them in this system) will go bad, being false signals of a trend. The other third will go along more or less well. Assuming the trending trade continues, the question for the campaign strategist is how to consolidate and then extend the thrust that is under way.

That thrust is the advance in equity, not the advance of the tradable. It's easy to stop at this point and think only of the trade that's on: "How's it doing? Are we up?" This is not the campaigner's point of view. In campaign trading, you think, "I've got a trade that appears, to date, to be good. If it turns out to be an extended move, which is the best thing possible, how can I prepare to exploit it fully? How can I build my equity most efficiently using this possible trend?"

The campaigner's approach is a far more complicated question than "Are we up?" It deals with

1. the likely rate of advance or decline
2. the likely duration of the advance or decline
3. the opportunities for add-on trades
4. the opportunities for countertrades

A campaigner expects tactical reversals even during a successful underlying trend trade. It's rare that an exchange-traded security goes straight up or down for an extended period of time given uncertainty, profit taking, and other possible factors. Although these retreats will be a setback for the original position, the campaigner will use firm, objective rules to assess whether each retreat is a reversal or an opportunity to add another position.

WHAT'S CHEAP, WHAT'S DEAR?

For the sake of simplicity, let's use an advance as an example.

If prices were going up, we would want to buy when things were cheap; if prices were going down, we'd sell when things were rich.

From a campaign standpoint, any of a number of ideas could be employed to gauge what's rich and what's cheap: retracement levels, detrended ranges, Elliott waves, swings, channels, and many others. For example, if you decide a 4% retracement in an uptrend is a good trading level, you could place an additional long as straightforwardly as a commander would throw reserves into the line as it sags under attack. As it happens, averages give an excellent indication of cheap or rich if you recall the skimming idea.

In this idea, we specifically picked averages that tended to skim along the bottoms of advances and the tops of declines. We did this visually (though more sophisticated techniques were available), and now it's time to exploit that behavior. For this job, averages are handier than trend lines because the rate of advance or decline automatically drives the average up or down at the appropriate slope. With drawn trend lines, we must initially guess what the slope of the trend line should be. Addicted chartists can still use trend lines in the manner I'm about to describe, but they'll work harder for less result.

Recall our having a longer moving average, intended to capture cyclical content up to 60 days, and a shorter average to capture near-term activity. Because the longer average reacts more slowly, it determines when we enter trend trades. Because it lags above or below the trend, it is also our lower or upper boundary for the trend, though we should keep in mind that prices need only stay flat for the average to catch up with them. If the average is our lower boundary during an advance, prices will be relatively cheap when they touch this average. At that point, we'll buy more. If we had entered a downtrend and prices rose to touch the long average, they would be relatively rich (relative to the prices in the trend) and therefore a good sell. Figure 5.1 shows how the moving average would look on the OEX for 1995's advance.

Looking at the OEX, note that additional positions are added when prices react to the longer average. An easy rule is to put in a buy stop at the estimated value of the average for the day, a value that can be extrapolated fairly closely from previous values of the average.

Note that these new positions from touching the longer average are not day-trades but additions to our underlying trend position.

If the short-term average has turned downward, kicking us out of our underlying long while the long average continues to rise, these touch points are only setups, places where we expect the opportunity to reenter. Ideally, we are long and looking to get longer when prices react to the longer average. We have the opportunity to add positions at favorable prices.

Just as a longer average like the traditional 21 days was used in Figure 5.1, a shorter average (5 days) may be used as well. By blowing up the March–June segment we can see many more trading activities. Every time the prices touch the five-day average we have an intraday trading opportunity, an opportunity that very occasionally turns into an additional trend position when the market rockets away from the average in our direction. Figure 5.2

FIGURE 5.1 OEX, 1995. ADD-ON TRADES USING 21-DAY SIMPLE MOVING AVERAGE. Form fitted for discussion, the 21-day and 5-day moving averages skim along the bottom of the OEX advance in 1995. One campaign tactic is to add to an advancing or declining trend trade by using moving averages to define cheap or rich entry points.

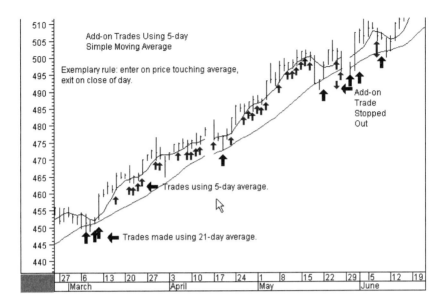

FIGURE 5.2 OEX, 1995. DAY-TRADING OPPORTUNITIES. ADD-ON TRADES USING 5–DAY SIMPLE MOVING AVERAGE. A shorter average designed to skim the bottoms or tops of advances or declines defines the lower boundary of the 1995 advance in the OEX. Traders enter on a buy stop set at the average's estimated value and exit at the close or a set profit level.

shows one form-fitted example from the 1995 bull market in equities. These are day trades, though. They exit on the close of the day of entry.

Intraday Trades

From a campaigner's point of view, these daily skirmishes should be a way of building capital and probing for weakness. Sometimes, when you send out a patrol in the form of a day-trade, you're aiming to get out of action at the end of the day, and you get your wish: a quick, small profit. Sometimes you run into an opposing patrol and you're lucky to disengage without casualty. Once in a while, the opposition comes at you in force just as you step out, steamrolling your trade and turning it into a loss. Whatever happens, it's the losses we're worried about. How big a loss does it take to convince us that our little day-trade is running into major opposition?

For example, using Figure 5.2, we go long as the price drifts down during the day to touch the short moving average's value. We expect that the moving average's value will act as a value reference point—support—and that the close, where we'll exit, will be higher. If that works out, fine. If not, we're looking at adverse price movement. We must cut that off somewhere and then let prices decline further until they reach the longer average, at which point we have another decision point. Therefore, as prices break below the five-day average, we'll have a loss when we stop out; that's the cost of trading. We want to keep those costs low, though.

Whether approaching probing day-trades or position-building trades, the important thing is not the entry rules that any imaginative trader could dream up. The first thing to do is look at the adverse price movement for each specific rule just as we did for the basic trend trade.

For each entry that follows the rules for entry and exit, we measure the adverse price movement to see how bad things get. Then we plot the distribution of adverse movements and see if there is a distinct difference between winners and losers. In other words, *for this distinct class of trades*[1] we analyze the results of our decision in the same manner we analyzed the results of our trend decision. We want a qualitative picture of those results, a picture we can use to cut off our losses efficiently and effectively.

Applying these two exploitations to Crude oil on a monthly basis for ten years generates a lot of trades. Let's take a look at the MAE distributions and the distributions of profit versus stop levels

---

[1] I highlight these words for the statisticians among us and those concerned with the number of rules used to generate out sample distributions. I argue that these add-on trades are independent of the underlying trend trade and that they need to be analyzed and financed independently.

I do not advocate adding trades by financing them with profits from the underlying trend trade, the practice of "pyramiding."

for New York Light Crude. First we'll do it for the position-building trades, then for the probing day-trades. If there is a distinct difference in the behavior of winning and losing trades, we'll have profits from (1) the underlying trade, (2) the add-on position trades, and (3) the day-trades in trend.

Probing Day Trades

One form of add-on trading uses the pricing that touches the short-term average. In this case, we know we're going to take more losses than if we traded prices touching the longer average. After all, every time the price went to the longer average's value, it had to first go *through* the shorter average's value, generating a loss. The adverse excursion information we generate should tell us if there's any distinction in our winning and losing trades when we trade off the short-term average and whether there is a logical place to put a stop based on experience.

To show that the experience with this different set of trading rules is consistent, I'm showing all ten years' graphs (see Figures 5.3 through 5.13). This is to demonstrate again that the phenomenon of distinct differences in distributions of losing trades versus those of winning trades exists and also to show you the variety and failures of this type of analysis. After, all nothing is perfectly consistent, and as you'll see, the market throws a lot of different conditions at us.

The trading rule used for these charts was that (1) an underlying trend trade was under way, (2) a buy or sell stop was placed at the day's projected value for the shorter average (12 days), and (3) the trade was closed at the end of the day.

Before showing the charts for other years, it's worth looking at the MAE chart and profitability charts for 1984 (Figure 5.3). The MAE chart has a very sharp distinction between winners and losers: there are no winners at all with an adverse price movement during the trade of more than sixteen ticks, or .16. Losers have larger adverse pricing, and one of the adverse movements is as much as 105 ticks, or over $1,000. Whether your stop could be exe-

FIGURE 5.3

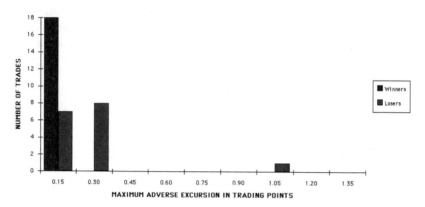

WINNERS AND LOSERS, 1984 ADD-ON TRADES FROM SHORT MOVING AVERAGE. Even on the short-term trades, winners simply don't have that much adverse excursion. They can be traded here with a stop of only 16 ticks, perhaps less.

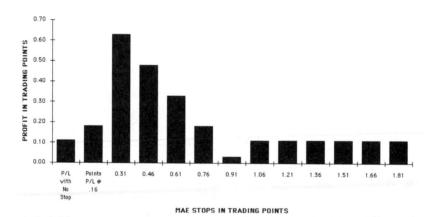

PROFITABILITY, 1984 ADD-ON TRADES. This chart deserves some thought. How could a stop of .31 have been more profitable than a stop of .16 if using .31 allowed additional losers. See the text for the answer.

FIGURE 5.3   (*Continued*)

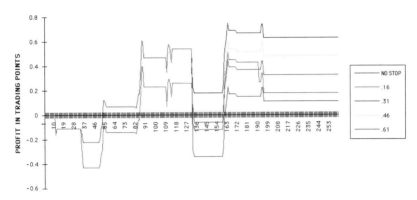

EQUITY LINES FOR VARIOUS STOP, 1984 ADD-ON TRADES. The stop of .31 shows the greatest profitability not from greater gains but lesser losses.

cuted in a market moving that far in a single day is certainly a question, but there's no protection at all without the stop that might have prevented that sort of loss.

Still, the 1984 profitability graph shows that a stop of .31 is more profitable than a stop of .16 even though no winners at all had an MAE greater than .16. How can that be? Well, what if a trade closed at a loss of .03 (3 ticks) but had an MAE of 20 ticks? With no stop, the equity line just goes down 3 ticks. With a stop of .16, the stop is hit and the equity line goes down 16 ticks. With a stop of .31, it goes down again just 3 ticks because the stop is not hit.

In 1984, this happened repeatedly: the closer stop caused more, larger losses than a more distant stop, as stops have been defined here. In other words, a stop too close converts some small losers into somewhat bigger losers. The effect of this must constantly be balanced against the benefit of the elimination of the huge losers.

The more conservative among us can still stop out profitably at .16. A more aggressive analyst can analyze the volatility that's showing large MAE with small losses on the close to decide if reaching for the extra profit is consistently worthwhile. For a clue, let's look at 1985 (Figure 5.4) and 1986 (Figure 5.5).

(*text continues on page 129*)

FIGURE 5.4

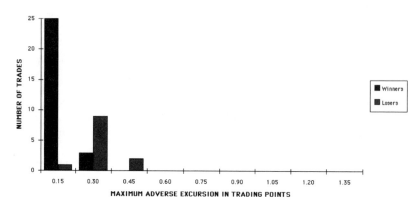

WINNERS AND LOSERS, 1985 ADD-ON TRADES FROM SHORT AVERAGE. 1985's distribution of losers again peaks in the .31 bin while winners peak in the first bin. The consistency of this distinction is always checked first to see if a new trading scheme is viable.

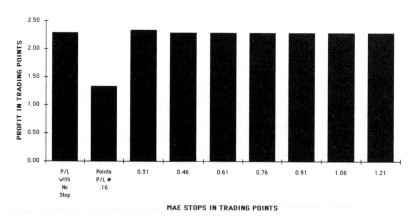

PROFITABILITY, 1985 SHORT-TERM ADD-ON TRADES. As in 1984, the trader must choose between a very safe but lower level of profitability with a close (.16) stop, or a higher risk and higher reward with a stop at .31.

FIGURE 5.4 (*Continued*)

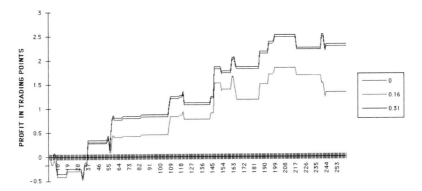

EQUITY LINES FOR VARIOUS STOPS, 1985 SHORT-TERM AVERAGE ADD-ON TRADES. 1985 did not have a horrendous loss to deal with so its equity line is smoother.

FIGURE 5.5

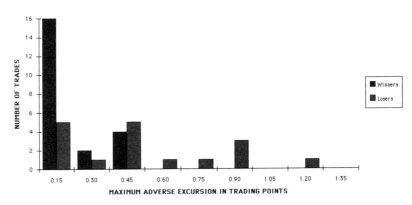

WINNERS AND LOSERS, 1986 ADD-ON TRADES FROM SHORT MOVING AVERAGE. 1986 offered many day-trades off the short-term average. The four winners with large adverse movements and the load of losers give a very jagged profit graph.

FIGURE 5.5   (*Continued*)

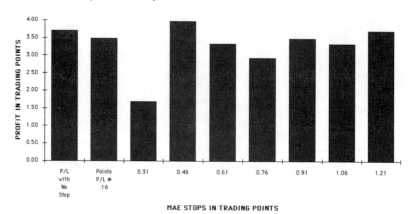

MAE STOPS IN TRADING POINTS

PROFITABILITY, 1986 SHORT-TERM ADD-ON TRADES. The ideal stop
level for this book's example—.31—takes the biggest hit in 1986.
Market perversity dictates that no one solution will be ideal for all
periods. Given the relative consistency of the other stop levels, the low
value at .31 is probably a random event.

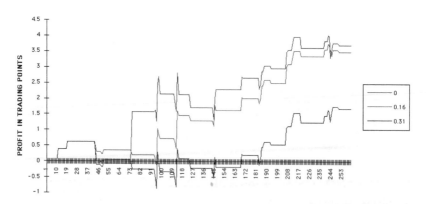

**EQUITY LINES FOR VARIOUS STOPS, 1986 SHORT-TERM AVERAGE
ADD-ON TRADES.**

FIGURE 5.6

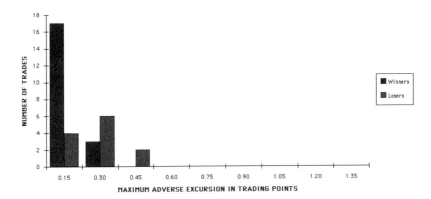

**WINNERS AND LOSERS, 1987 ADD-ON TRADES FROM SHORT
MOVING AVERAGE.** 1987 shows a good distinction between winners
and losers, with winners having very little adverse excursion.
Profitability grows as stops are widened to .3.

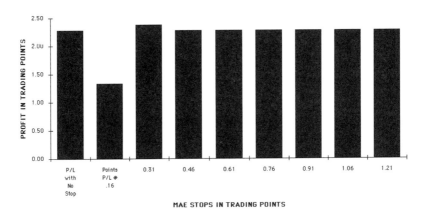

PROFITABILITY, 1987 SHORT-TERM ADD-ON TRADES.

FIGURE 5.6   (*Continued*)

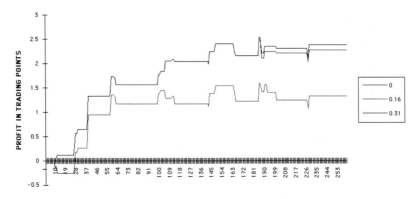

EQUITY LINES FOR VARIOUS STOPS, 1987 SHORT-TERM ADD-ON TRADES.

FIGURE 5.7

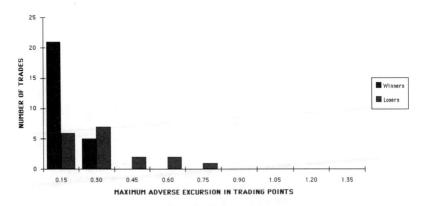

WINNERS AND LOSERS, 1988 ADD-ON TRADES FROM SHORT MOVING AVERAGE. 1988 typifies one attractive feature of add-on day-trades: a high percentage of winners.

FIGURE 5.7   (*Continued*)

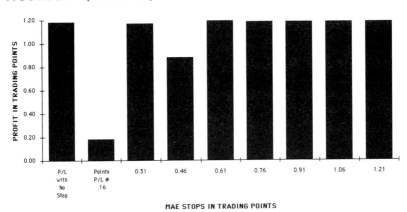

PROFITABILITY, 1988 SHORT-TERM ADD-ON TRADES.

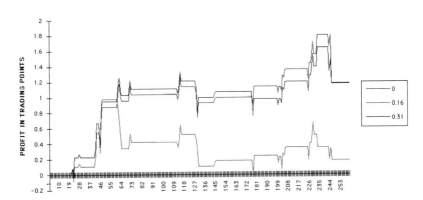

EQUITY LINES FOR VARIOUS STOPS, 1988 SHORT-TERM ADD-ON
TRADES. Stops at .3 give the 1988 trades enough room to flourish, apparently just outside the noise range of the data that year. Losers had much larger adverse excursions.

FIGURE 5.8

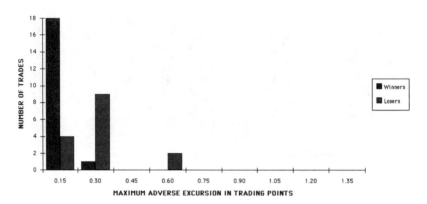

WINNERS AND LOSERS, 1989 ADD-ON TRADES FROM SHORT MOVING AVERAGE. A stop at .16 might be tempting based on the MAE chart, but the profitability chart shows the .3 level is as good as in previous years and significantly more profitable.

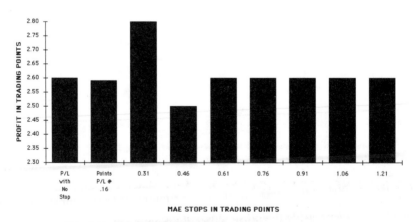

PROFITABILITY, 1989 SHORT-TERM ADD-ON TRADES.

FIGURE 5.8 (*Continued*)

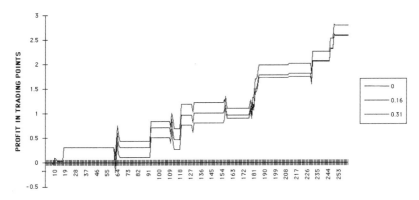

EQUITY LINES FOR VARIOUS STOPS, 1989 SHORT-TERM ADD-ON TRADES.

FIGURE 5.9

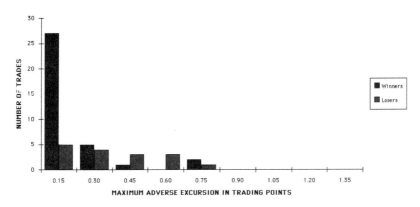

WINNERS AND LOSERS, 1990 ADD-ON TRADES FROM SHORT MOVING AVERAGE. 1990 MAE. This is a unique graph: the distribution of winners extends its tail as far as that of the losers. For more on the results from the tumultuous years of 1990 and 1991, see the 1990 profitability and equity charts and Figure 5.10.

FIGURE 5.9   (*Continued*)

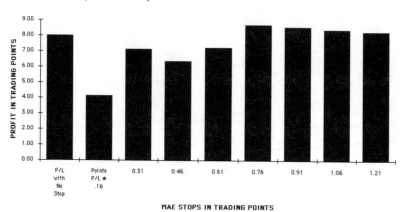

MAE STOPS IN TRADING POINTS

PROFITABILITY, 1990 SHORT-TERM ADD-ON TRADES. Despite amazing daily swings, any of the stop strategies kept you in the game and reaping profits from market actions.

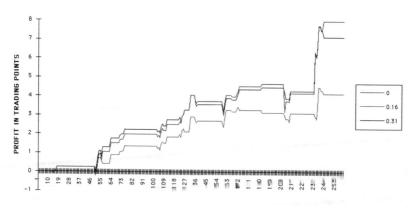

EQUITY LINES FOR VARIOUS STOPS, 1990 SHORT-TERM ADD-ON TRADES.

FIGURE 5.10

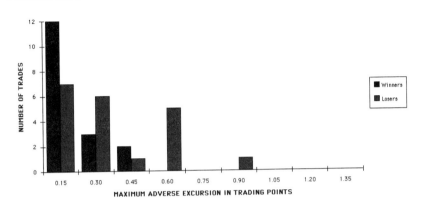

WINNERS AND LOSERS, 1991 ADD-ON TRADES FROM SHORT
MOVING AVERAGE. 1991 profitability. MAE fails to perform miracles in the wild ride of 1991. Add-on trades suffer their only losing year in the volatility surrounding the Gulf War.

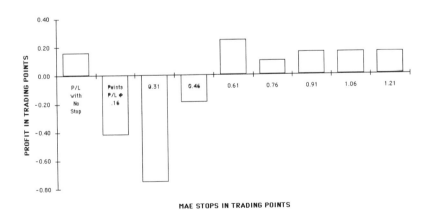

PROFITABILITY, 1991 SHORT-TERM ADD-ON TRADES.

FIGURE 5.10   (*Continued*)

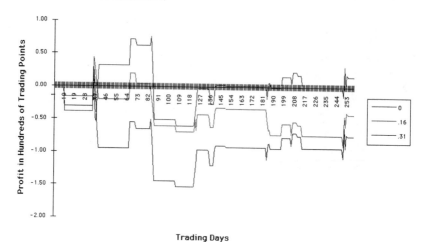

Trading Days

EQUITY LINES FOR VARIOUS STOPS, 1991 SHORT-TERM ADD-ON TRADES.

FIGURE 5.11

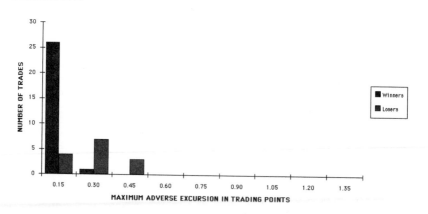

WINNERS AND LOSERS, 1992 ADD-ON TRADES FROM SHORT MOVING AVERAGE. This year is one of the few to date where a stop tighter than .3 would have been more effective. The very low adverse excursion for winners causes this result.

FIGURE 5.11 (*Continued*)

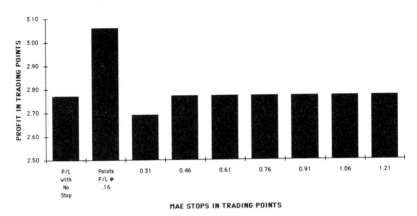

MAE STOPS IN TRADING POINTS

PROFITABILITY, 1992 SHORT-TERM ADD-ON TRADES.

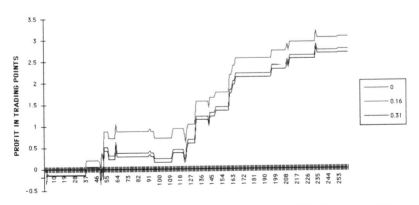

EQUITY LINES FOR VARIOUS STOPS, 1992 SHORT-TERM ADD-ON
TRADES.

FIGURE 5.12

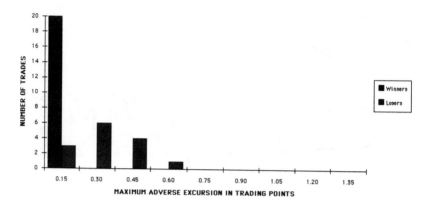

WINNERS AND LOSERS, 1993 ADD-ON TRADES FROM SHORT
MOVING AVERAGE.

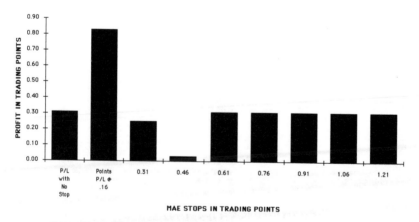

PROFITABILITY, 1993 SHORT-TERM ADD-ON TRADES.

FIGURE 5.12 *(Continued)*

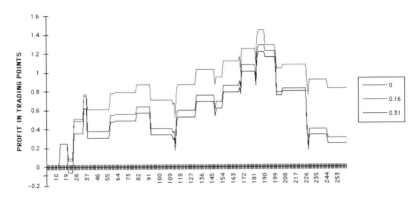

EQUITY LINES FOR VARIOUS STOPS, 1993 SHORT-TERM ADD-ON TRADES. 1993 equity line. Nearby stops save most of the year's profitability in contrast to 1984's experience where they cost money. Such contrasting results are inevitable with any hard and fast rules.

FIGURE 5.13

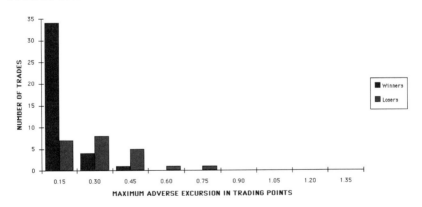

WINNERS AND LOSERS, 1994 ADD-ON TRADES FROM SHORT MOVING AVERAGE. The .3 stop level again plays a better result after two years doing worse than the .15 level. Switching to .15 would have resulted in lower profits this year.

FIGURE 5.13   (*Continued*)

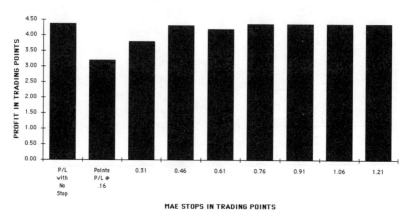

PROFITABILITY, 1994 SHORT-TERM ADD-ON TRADES.

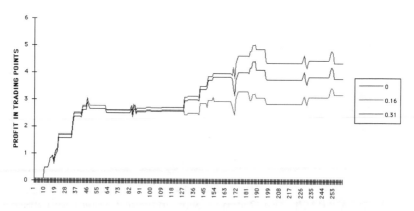

EQUITY LINES FOR VARIOUS STOPS, 1994 SHORT-TERM ADD-ON TRADES.

Inspection of Figures 5.4 through 5.13 should give you an idea of the variety of experience you'll face in the market once you view it through the lens of your trading rules. The 1984–1994 charts certainly show profitability and they show the impact of using the MAE technique to manage losses. The trading rules here are far from the most complicated that could be devised, and the years have a wide variety of trading experiences, yet each year shows how, given these trading rules, losses can be minimized and equity grown with a straightforward technique.

As you can see, there is plenty of variety in the results, so some summation would be nice. Figure 5.14 is the summary table of trades with various MAEs for Crude using the trading of the nearby active months for 1984–1994.

To summarize eleven years' experience day-trading the short-term moving average, this approach has a higher win—loss ratio than the underlying trend trade, and trades more frequently for smaller gains but greater total profitability (see Figure 5.15).

From the standpoint of the campaigner, this low-margin activity (positions aren't held overnight) can significantly exploit a trend

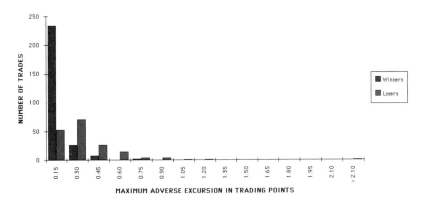

FIGURE 5.14   MAE FOR ADD-ON TRADES. WINNERS AND LOSERS, SHORT AVERAGE ADD-ON TRADES, 1984–1994. The high percentage of winners is the most comforting feature of add-on day-trades. Next best is the sharp distinction in the two distributions, which should allow a good choice in a stop.

FIGURE 5.15 PROFITABILITY OF SHORT AVERAGE ADD-ON TRADES, 1984–1994. Risk gets its reward in the ten-year compilation. As you cut losses by using stops, profits drop. As stops are relaxed, profits rise.

with manageable losses. Just looking at the results with no stops indicates that, in this peculiar case, this type of add-on trade is a sensible strategy with solid profitability. While it doesn't build a bigger underlying position, it does build the campaigner's strength for the main push. Now the campaign has two things going for it: the trend trade and intraday add-on trades.

Position-Building Trades

Because the longer average turns upward last (usually, though not necessarily), its direction is really the defining feature of trending as it's defined in this book. Now we want to see what the results are of adding on trades when prices hit the longer average.

The trading rule used in this test was that (1) an underlying trend trade was under way, (2) a buy or sell stop was placed at the day's projected value[2] for the longer average, and (3) each trade was

---

[2] Any imaginative analyst can look at a series of moving-average values and come up with a good estimate of the next value. I usually extend the five-day trend of changes to the change from today to calculate tomorrow's value.

closed at the end of the underlying trade.[3] Trades were entered
when the low or high exceeded the average's value by two or more
points.[4]

To spare you all the charts from each year, Figures 5.16 and 5.17
summarizes the 1984–1994 position-building trades.

It's tough to make too much of these results because there are
very few trades during the ten-year period. Some years there were
no trades at all—the market just ran away from the long-term
trend line. Some years there was only one. Analytically, there
aren't enough trades even to have confidence that the distributions are exemplary, even though they look familiar: the losing
distribution with a long tail and the winners clustered around the
Y axis.

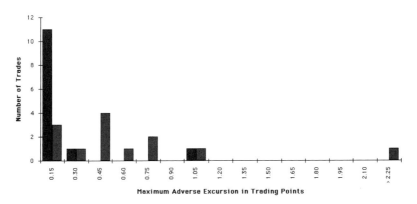

**FIGURE 5.16   MAE FOR POSITION ADD-ONS. WINNERS AND
LOSERS VS. MAE, 1984–1994.** There aren't many chances to add on
trades to your underlying position using the logic in this system, but
even with distinct trading rules, the winners' adverse movement is much
less than losers'. This makes possible some artful stop placement.

---

[3] Later we'll look more closely at the issue of exiting. For now, our exit is defined
by the rules of the trend trade.

[4] Because the extreme prices of the day have only a trade or two, it's more realistic
to try to enter a couple ticks away from the extreme recorded in the price data.

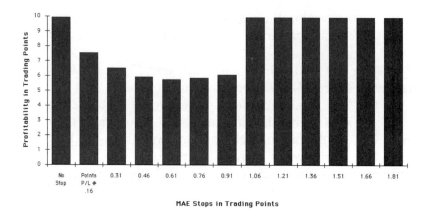

FIGURE 5.17   PROFIT FROM POSITION ADD-ONS. PROFITABILITY VS. MAE, 1984–1994. Here's a unique case where wider stops, on comparatively few trades, show lower profitability even as more risk is accepted. Only if the stop is virtually ineffective does higher reward match the higher risk.

This is "real world." You don't get textbook clarity in the data and you have to make decisions on indications and insufficient data. Personally, I'd be comfortable trading from this because I'm comfortable that these distributions crop up wherever consistent rules apply. You might say, "Forget it! I'm not going to make add-on trades to the longer trend. The data just aren't there." These are decisions traders make in an uncertain world.

The profitability distribution shown in Figure 5.17 demonstrates that using stops reduces overall profitability. Lower potential for loss means lower profit. It is unusual, though, that as the stop is widened from .16 to 1.06, profits decline slowly. Given the low number of trades we're working with here, I don't attribute much significance to this. I'd be comfortable putting my stop anywhere in the range from .16 to .61 (the 2% or $600 limit on position losses). Again, purely from the convenience of using two contracts instead of one, a stop at .31 would work as well as prevent any catastrophic losses.

SUMMARY PROFITABILITY

We've now tested three ways of trading, and our campaign is only in the trend mode so far, Table 5.1 shows how the three combine in impact.

From a campaigner's standpoint, we've developed three methods, each more or less successful, to exploit trending behavior. The cumulative profitability of the campaign is beginning to build and therefore our trading strength. This is the effect we seek in the campaign: a gradual accretion of strength and power.

I don't claim that these particular rules are the best but I will vouch for the process of testing to limit losses and estimate profit levels. That the MAE process is unusual shouldn't be a deterrent. It addresses the core problems of any trading operation and, so far, has been successful for three different sets of trading rules. That testing could be applied to any other set of rules you could imagine.

For example, how about trading against the trend? When or how could that make sense? Ideas about the channel of a trend are common so, if you'd defined a channel, prices would be rich at the upper side of an uptrend's channel and cheap at the lower side of a downtrend's channel. You'd sell at the extremes, as illustrated in Figure 5.18.

As far as the campaigner is concerned, the question is, no matter how perilous the idea, how would it test out? That is, how much adverse price movement would be expected for a winning trade and how much for a losing trade? Just from Figure 5.18 we can see we'd miss some trades and suffer adverse prices on others. Rather than

TABLE 5.1   CAMPAIGN TRADING PROFITABILITY NEW YORK LIGHT CRUDE, 1984–1994.

Mode	Rule	Stop Level	Profit/Loss
Trend	Two moving averages	.31	3600
Trend	Add-on day trades	.31	2500
Trend	Add-on position trades	.31	640

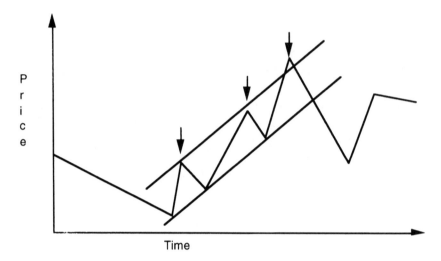

FIGURE 5.18   COUNTERTRADING. Here's an idea: countertrading against the trend. Not something many are comfortable doing, it's still a technique that can be tested with the MAE process to see if it makes sense.

just stick with the trend trade, or just stick with the add-on trades, we can evaluate countertrading too, with the same loss-limiting technique. If it makes money under our loss limitations, we tack it into our campaign's list of tactics.

What wouldn't make sense? It wouldn't make sense to use counter-trading if there were no difference between the distributions of MAE for winning and losing trades. That would mean the rules we'd selected just could not distinguish between winning trades and losing trades. Although the distributions can be distinguished in statistical terms of median, skew, and kurtosis[5] traders will skip all that and eyeball the situation. Because there's no need to push it (there being lots of trading situations and trading rules), an am-biguous distinction from one set of trading rules should simply be rejected. Move on to another set of rules.

---

[5] Skew is the amount of lean to one side or another that a distribution has. Kurto-sis is the "peakedness" of a distribution.

SUMMARY

Exploit a trend with additional entries to take advantage of the underlying movement of the tradable. The goal is to build your strength and the basic trend position. The rules you select don't make a lot of difference as long as the losses are controlled adequately with MAE stops. For example, we tested three simple rules and found all, adequately stopped, contributed to profitability. Many other ideas and rules could be tested.

6

Reversing Bad Trades

The campaigning trader has taken three looks at the market already but doesn't stop there. Are there other aspects of trending that can be exploited? What about nontrending periods? Is there some other market mode that can be defined and exploited? In other words, the trader is always looking for another avenue to trade, to build equity. Here's another.

Our logic on trending trades was that, if we're right, the trade won't go very far against us. As we've seen, this isn't perfect, but in the aggregate, it works out. Also, as the biggest benefit, this cuts off some trades that would otherwise go way in the hole. What if instead of just cutting off some of those losers we turned around and rode them?

In this chapter, we'll explore this idea conceptually before testing it. The idea of reversing is generally worth keeping in mind. Later, when we're working on channel breakouts, the breakout will be defined by a reversal. The manner in which the reversal or breakout is defined will be the same as defined in this chapter.

This idea may seem a little off the wall to some. After all, the trend indicators are by definition headed in one direction, and we're talking about taking trades in the other direction. However, this is simply "getting right with the market," "admitting you're wrong," or "turning on a dime." This chapter discusses a rational way for the campaigner to do this difficult chore.

THE IDEA

It won't take much inspection of the charts in Chapter 4 to find several years with large adverse excursions, price movements in the "wrong" direction that were cut off with MAE stops. Nearly always, these were eventually losing trades under the trending rules. If they were going to be losers (and going past our MAE stop made that probability about 90%), why not turn them into winners? After all, what's the risk? The risk would be if they eventually turned into winners for the original trade—which we estimate is a 10% probability.[1] In 10% of the cases, we'll cut off an eventual winner by reversing, but in 90% of the cases, the amount that can be lost is *our original MAE stop amount.*[2] That amount is well within our capital constraint guideline, and if that's the case, this is an idea worth exploring.

When you think about it, there are really only three outcomes to a trade entry: favorable, unfavorable, or no action. (You could cut that to two if you wanted analytical rigor.) These results are depicted in Figure 6.1.

Profitable Trade (Line A)

Looking at Figure 6.1, first focus on line A. This is the hoped-for result, and it measures how much profit the position holds measured from the point of entry. It's all in the black here and ends when there is a sharp reversal in the market, causing a drop in profit and an end to the trade according to our trading rules. In this book, it would be the reversal of one of the two averages, probably the short-term average.

This reversal establishes the trade horizon, the period of time during which our logic will hold. It's the period of time defined by our underlying trend-trading rules. In this book's example, it's

---

[1] You can adjust these ratios by your place of the stop on the original MAE trade. To go from 90% to 95%, for example, you'd widen the stop at the cost of larger losses from stops and the benefit of fewer winners being stopped out.

[2] Why? Because otherwise it would have ended up a winner in the first place.

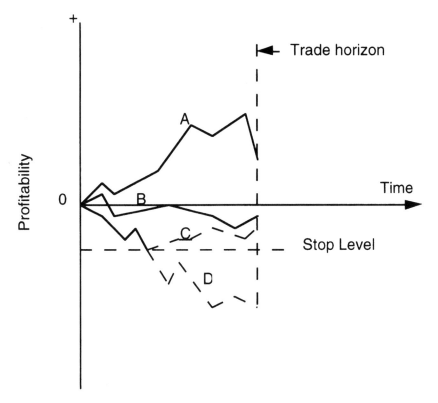

FIGURE 6.1   PROFITABILITY SINCE INCEPTION. Trades go favorably, unfavorably, or nowhere in this depiction of the profit or loss measured from entry. Trades that hit the stop are candidates for reversal because there is a low probability they will return to profitability.

when both averages are headed up or down. It's during this period that we have some information about what a good trade will do and what a bad trade will do, particularly the latter. (That information was the trend trading in Chapter 4.)

Goes Nowhere (Line B)

Another possibility for traders is that the trade will essentially go nowhere. Where movement was expected, none occurs. This is line

B, here carried out to the trade horizon's boundary for consistency's sake. Here, we're probably in a trading range, though whether it's tradable is a subject for a later chapter.

A Loser That Comes Back (Line C)

Third, a trade could go bad. It would wander down to the stop and hit it. Or it could be one of those few winners we chose to cut off by our selection of the MAE stop. If, for some irrational reason, we didn't stop out at the MAE stop, it would rebound. Line C is the line of hope wherein losses turn into profits or are at least minimized.

Fat chance!

Depending on the distribution of adverse price movement for the losers, it may have a sharply higher chance or only a slightly higher chance, but one thing is nearly certain: once it hits the stop, the chances that it would have been a winning trade are as minimal as we've chosen to make it by our stop placement for the original trend trade. We've chosen a stop that is specifically designed to distinguish between winners and losers. If this trade were to be a winner, it's unlikely given our measured experience that it would have hit the stop in the first place. No, this trade is likely a loser and the question is: how much of a loser?

According to Figure 6.2, if we set the stop at .31 the estimated probability of still being a winner on the original trade is 12/101 or about 12%. In other words, from .31 south there are 12 winners we've cut off (in ten years) and 89 losers. Note that some of those 89 losers went *way* into the hole. We want to get some of that price movement into our equity account.

A Reversal Trade (Line D)

If the underlying trade has a low probability of profitability (12%) having hit the .31 stop, it also has an apparently high probability (88%) of going further bad (line D)? *Turning things around* now, if we reverse the original trade we would have an upside potential of from .31 to over 2.10 and a downside of .31, keeping in mind that

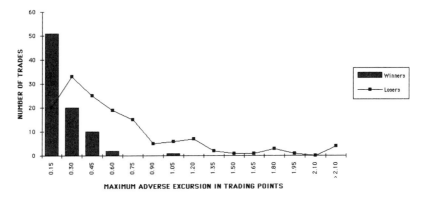

FIGURE 6.2   MAE USING MONTHLY CONTRACTS. Winners and losers versus MAE, 1984–1994.

12 underlying winning trades, if reversed, will become losers. This is potentially favorable and so merits some investigation.

TRADING RULES

If long or short, place a reversing stop (sell or buy two contracts or blocks of stock) at .31 trading points. For the initial analysis of the reversal strategy, place no protective stop. Exit on the end-of-trade date for the underlying trade.

Did you forget about the trade horizon? Because all our information about trade behavior takes place within the trading horizon established by the underlying trade's rules, we must continue to track its status. If we're long, we have until one or the other of the averages goes down. If we're short, one or the other of the averages will break upward, indicating the period of the underlying trade is over. At this point, we'll exit the reversal trade just as we would have exited the underlying trade.

RESULTS

Following these trading rules, Figure 6.3 shows the results using the eleven years of Crude data, rolling every month to the most active contract.

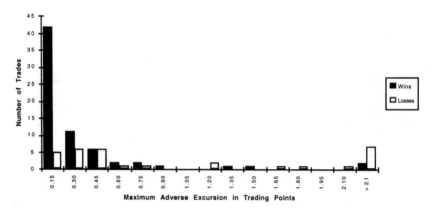

FIGURE 6.3   REVERSAL MAE. Winners and losers versus MAE, 1984–1994. Compared to the underlying trend system, reversal trades have a very high success rate even with simple exit rules. Limitations of the data exaggerate the size of the MAEs for winners.

The most striking thing shown by Figure 6.3 is the heavy dominance of the winning category. Winners occurred 68 times to 31 losers, even with a naive exit scheme. There aren't many trading schemes that offer a 70% success rate but there are still sobering thoughts regarding this:

1. Keep in mind you had to eat a loss of 31 ticks on the underlying trend trade to get to the winner. That amount is tallied in your profit/loss statement for the trend trading, though, which was profitable despite it.
2. The distributions are much more similar than they were for the underlying trade. Both winning and losing distributions have long tails. What could that mean?
3. There are some huge MAEs for winning trades. Why?
4. What is the overall profitability if stops are used?

INSPECTION

Stepping through the experience of the actual trades is extremely valuable. Although the process can be automated, you learn something by seeing what happens trade by trade. As you see each trade progress day by day, Crude shows several typical market behaviors at the times when reversals are triggered, behaviors that I've lumped into descriptive categories. I've done this to show that reversal trading is not always "getting right with the trend." That happens, but it's more complex than it seems and takes two steps: (1) reversal out of the original mistake and (2) initiation of a trend trade. Figure 6.4 shows the types of trades I encountered while watching Crude reversal trades.

Mistaken Reversals

Days in underlying trend trade before reversing: one or two. Days in reversal trade: seven or more.

In these trades, the reversal catches the underlying trend trade's stop and triggers by just two or three ticks. This is the thing traders hate the most, especially in the 11 cases (11%) here where the reversal trades went on to become losers, sometimes serious losers. Not only do you convert winning trend trades to losers, but you make the loss bigger by reversing.

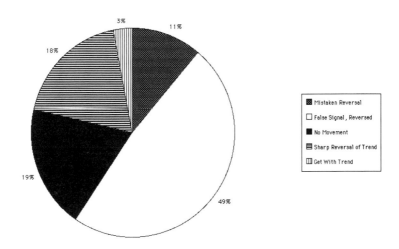

FIGURE 6.4   CATEGORIES OF REVERSAL TRADES. About half the reversals done in Crude from 1984–1994 were of false trend signals. These usually happened quickly: in and out in two or three days.

In these data, trades are typified by entry soon after the start of the underlying trade (1 or 2 days) and then a long run (7 to 35 days) going the wrong direction. These trades are the source of the long tails in Figure 6.3. Thankfully, this is a rare experience, though living through it is not fun. It should be rare because we selected the trend trade's MAE stop to make it rare. Having selected the stop, though, we should keep in mind that it's not perfect. We're playing experience, and experience is not a perfect guide to the future.

Getting Right with the Market

Especially if the stop has been picked by just a few points, we may need to reverse again to get right with the market. The problem analytically is that there aren't enough of these situations to define rules for MAE stops. Frankly, we are thrown back on judgment.

In Figure 6.5, the logic of our original reversal idea is that if a reversal trade were to back up .31, the trade might be one of those trend winners we cut out with an MAE stop (line A). This isn't foolproof because all we know from experience is that at the *end* of the trade horizon, 12% of the winning trades will have experienced an MAE greater than .31 and come back into the black. If a trend trade goes back to zero (which would be an adverse excursion of .31 from the reversal trade's entry), it could happen *at any time* during the trend trade's horizon.

The other alternative shown in Figure 6.5 is line B, a trade that touches the adverse excursion stop and then retreats back to zero before ending as a loss. Without intraday data and enough trades to do an analysis, we can't develop trading rules supported by quantitative observation. This is a limitation of MAE analysis and the amount of data you have.

False (Trend) Signal, Quickly Reversed

Days in underlying trade: one or two. Days in reversal trade: zero or one.

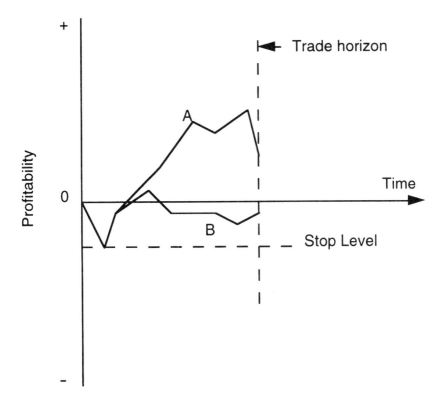

FIGURE 6.5   REVERSAL LOGIC. Some reversals are just plain mistakes. The difficulty is in distinguishing between an eventual trend winner (A) and a loser (B), which both wander back and forth across the original point of entry.

These are great: the original trend trade is just plain wrong, and the market breaks decisively in the other direction immediately. Keeping in mind that these reversal trades were ended *when the underlying trend trade stopped*, sharp reversals were most commonly quick trades. Moreover, because the market action was sharp enough to end the trend trade, it is often sharp enough to trigger a sharp move, one whose profitability is not caught by these trading rules. The reversals force closure within two days and often end the trend trade the same day. Nearly half the trades (48) were this type.

These were generally profitable and served to make up some of the losses from the underlying trade.

Unfortunately, we don't see the full extent of the profits from these trades in this data because the reversal trades are closed at the end of the underlying trade. This means we are closing out a trade that is headed in the correct direction. Also, the underlying trade would reverse itself immediately or soon thereafter and go on to glory.

It seems that once you hit the MAE stop in Crude, the best guess is that the market is going to go in the other direction.

No Movement

Days in underlying trade before reversal: three or more. Days in reversal trade: three or more.

These 18 (19%) are trades that occur three or more days into the underlying trade and last for another three to ten days. The market is not moving enough to end the underlying trade, or the expiring data in the averages is moving so coincidentally with the new data that an end to the trend trade is not signaled.

Profitability on these trades is indifferent, with no great losses or profits.

Sharp Reversal of Trend

Days in underlying trade: three or more. Days in reversal trade: zero or one.

Here, a trade proceeds profitably for several days before in a single day, it reverses direction sharply, setting off the reversal trade and ending the underlying trade on the same day. Adverse excursion on these reversals is difficult to evaluate accurately using daily data because you don't have intraday information on maximum adverse excursion *after* the reversal trade is triggered. That's the day the reversal and the underlying trade most often end, so this is a warning.

In this data I have, by inspection of the opening, closes, and subsequent price action, judged the likely level of adverse excursion, if any. Those with intraday data can check more closely, though in my sampling I've found this a sterile exercise. In this exercise, there were 18 instances (18%) of sharp reversals.

Getting Right with the Trend

It's remarkable how seldom this happens (about three times in 99 reversal trades), but after all, our original trading system was designed to be right with the trend. If reversals did that job, it would be a real conceptual problem. What reversals actually do is get you out of a mistake (and occasionally into another), get you right with the reaction to a trend, or get you out of a trend trade that doesn't go anywhere.

Figure 6.6 points out that whatever trend with which we get right had better play out within five days and certainly no more

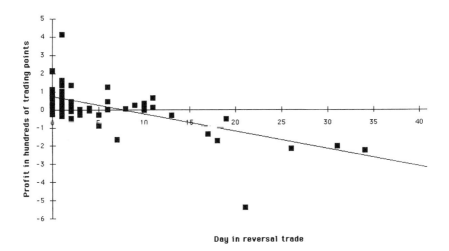

Day in reversal trade

FIGURE 6.6   PROFITABILITY VS. DAYS IN TRADE. Net profitability of reversal trades, 1984–1994. The longer you're in a reversal, the more dismal the results. Good things usually happen quickly, within two days.

than ten. All the profitability is concentrated in the first ten days of the reaction. Given that most reversing trades from trending are finished in two days, the variability of the result widens rapidly from three days on upward, as seen in Figure 6.6. These data suggest that a reversal trade that lasts more than two days is a very uncertain situation; beyond ten days it's almost certainly a loser.

Just to sharpen the point that reversals are fast and furious, look at Figure 6.7. The most common underlying trend trade lasts just a single day and is most commonly closed within the next day (zero days in the reversal trade). To restate that, about half the time a reversal is triggered, the underlying trend trade will have been put on yesterday. Today we get kicked out of it and reverse.

Furthermore, within five days, 80% of the reversals are finished, that is, half the time the reversals we do get will be over today and most of the rest will be done within five days. This just reinforces the lesson in Figure 6.6 that the reversals can be profitable quickly, recovering some or all of the losses experienced in reversing.

There also exists a rough reverse symmetry between days in the underlying trade and days in the reversal trade, as shown in Figure 6.8. For example, trades occurring only one day after the underly-

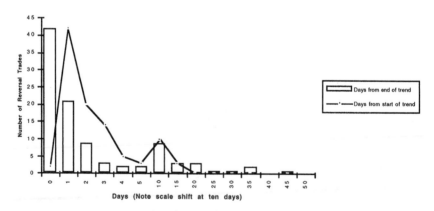

FIGURE 6.7   DAYS FROM BEGINNING OR END OF UNDERLYING TREND TRADE. Reversals that happen inside one day dominate the statistics. What's more, underlying trades generating reversals typically only last a single day.

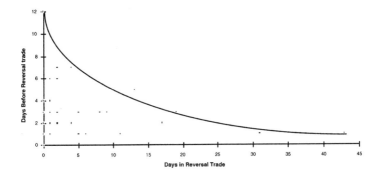

FIGURE 6.8   DAYS IN TRADE VS. DAYS BEFORE TRADE. Days in versus days before reversals entered on the first day of the underlying trade could last quite a while, but those entered late in the underlying's life are likely to be brief. Here the frontier of this relationship is drawn.

ing gets under way could go on for 35 days. (You probably got nicked with a spike downward of 32 ticks.) At the other extreme, a reversal triggered on the 12th day of the underlying, would be expected to last zero days—the underlying trade would end the same day.

PROFITABILITY OF REVERSING

Reversing from trend trades is generally profitable and low loss. Assuming the stop level is our original entry we assume only .31 of loss. Even after we absorb the 11% of trades that hit the trend MAE stop and went on to become winners (that is, they were big losers when reversed), reversal trading is probably comparable to add-ons as an additional source of profitability, as shown in Table 6.1.

Although reversal trading is profitable, its true impact is probably understated in Table 6.1. First, reversals that become trend trades are cut off when the original trend trade ends. Second, the trend winners that hit the trend MAE stop, if reversed again, would have contributed more profits. However, because there are too few of those to trust the sampling, I omit their results from a

**TABLE 6.1   CAMPAIGN TRADING PROFITABILITY,
NEW YORK LIGHT CRUDE, 1984–1994.**

Mode	Rule	Stop Level	Profit/Loss (points)
Trend	Two moving averages	.31	3600
Trend	Add-on day trades	.31	2500
Trend	Add-on position trades	.31	640
Trend	Reversal	.31	1827

tabulation. I do advocate your becoming familiar with them, though. Were I to reverse a trend trade on an MAE stop hit by just three or four ticks within a day or two, followed by a strong rebound in the original trend direction, I'd feel justified in reversing again with a loss potential of .31. This is just personal judgment of the Crude market. You'll make a conclusion based on your analysis and experience.

Another point about reversals: Because reversals, by definition, take you out of the trend trade, your capital requirement is not necessarily increased by reversing.[3] Add-on position trades, being separately capitalized, do tend to increase the total amount of capital required as large portfolios are assembled. For example, if trading only one item, it's hard to conceive of having 50 trades (100% ÷ 2%) on at the same time. On the other hand, if trading 200 items, you could easily have 100 trades on at one time. That would mean (if all have the same acceptable loss level) you'd need at least twice the capital you'd need in the first situation.

SUMMARY

If a trade hits our MAE stop, there's a high probability that, within our trading horizon, it will end up a loser. It may be that if we re-

_____

[3] Your capital requirement may be increased if your analysis of runs of trades indicates an uncomfortable probability that your capital could be reduced to the point that you couldn't undertake those reversal trades you need to complete your campaign of trading. This complex subject I leave to a more detailed treatment in a later book.

verse (say, short) and it ends up below our MAE stop level, some of the losses can be recovered. Of course, it may end up above the MAE stop level or even above the entry point for the underlying trend trade, in which case we eat a second loss. It all depends on where you've set the MAE stop level and the characteristic behavior of your market.

Reversing is an essential skill for a campaigning trader. A market will not always trend, so the inevitable bad trades must be handled gracefully so as to recover some of the losses with reversals. The willingness to reverse is a key sign that, psychologically, you're willing to win rather than be correct calling the market.

That said, it may be that the reversal strategy would not work with your tradable. You must do the analysis to make the trading rule. If it turns out to be viable, at least as far as experience goes, you add it to the campaign plan, which already includes trend trading and two kinds of add-on trades.

P
r
i
c
e

Time

7

Switching Modes: Trading Ranges

We've just spent six chapters on the most popular trading situation: trending. It's commonly said that most trading instruments aren't trending all the time or even most of the time. More objectively, we can tell from the number of reversal trades from false signals that our trend indicator is often wrong. While a truly active trader will constantly screen for trending behavior, shifting his vehicle as necessary, this book is about another approach: a concerted campaign to exploit fully one vehicle. To do that, we need to trade when our tradable isn't trending.

Every trend ends. In our example, the end came when the rules for exiting were tripped. One or the other of the averages broke step with its mate. It could have been any set of rules and the important thing was that it set the time horizon for our trading. Now that the trend trade (and any add-ons) are finished, what do we have?

For one thing, we might get a lot of chances to trade. Was the New York Light Crude market in trending mode only a third of the time?[1] Actually, no. For Crude, from 1984 to 1994, with the rules

---

[1] I couldn't resist checking this and found that "time in trend trade" was 50 + 102 + 161 + 145 + 137 + 150 + 189 + 177 + 132 + 123 + 164 = 1,530 of 2,800 days, or 55%.

we've used here the market was in a trend (i.e., one lasting more than three days) 55% of the time, a number I find surprisingly high. Nevertheless, there were periods when the trending indicator could not pick up meaningful advances or declines. Arbitrarily, I'm going to call these nontrending periods *trading ranges* and try to extract some money from them.

A campaign trader may expect to see ranging prices at the beginning of a trend rather than at the end of a trend. In physical commodities and stocks, there are often long basing periods before trends, situations that are best handled as trading ranges. However, in rates and currencies, particularly the former, ranges appearing after trends seem to be those preparatory to a new trend. Long-term basing seems uncommon in rates and currencies compared to stocks.

Wherever we look, the first problem will be to see the range forming in time to exploit it.

RECOGNIZING RANGING

If I showed a number of people three or four charts, nearly every person could probably pick out areas where the price was going nowhere over a period of time. (Refer, again, to the perception issue described in Chapter 2.) This perceptual phenomenon occurs whether we're looking at tick charts, daily, weekly, or month charts (see Figure 7.1). And, just for starters, I'm going to circle the areas I pick out.

However, to eventually get this idea of prices being relatively stable into a computer, I'll need to be more objective. Clearly lower lows/lower highs or higher highs/higher lows will not constitute a trading range. Prices must return to the approximate levels they achieved in some period before. Otherwise, the central value, if there is, one, is still moving upward or downward.

This return to a previous price level can be observed visually and by the computer. All the computer needs to know is how far back to look when making its comparison. As shown in Figure 7.2, if we

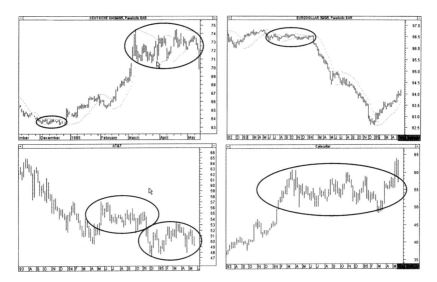

FIGURE 7.1   PICKING OUT RANGES. Ranging behavior crops up on all time scales, intraday to monthly. Picking it out visually usually isn't too difficult. Getting a computer to see what we see is tougher.

set that look-back period too short, it won't see the last low. If we set it too long, it might pick up a low six months ago.

How far back do we look? If we can see trading ranges on daily, weekly, monthly, or even five-minute charts, which one is relevant? This is where the time horizon discussed earlier comes into play.

Time Horizon

First, you've already chosen how often you'll monitor the market, usually looking at the data for entry signals. A retail speculator has the luxury of choosing his time frame: intraday, daily, weekly, bi-weekly and so on whereas, institutionally, the exigencies of serving customers or the business often dictate the trading horizon. Although there exist retail day-traders, most don't have the daytime

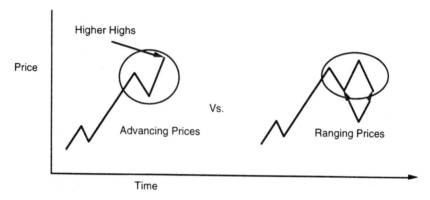

FIGURE 7.2   SIMPLE DEFINITION OF RANGING. The absence of higher highs with higher lows and the return to previous price levels is the first clue to ranging behavior. When we see this, we have a well-defined trade entry because a long will be quickly stopped out or be profitable to the other side of the range.

free, and the majority of them use daily prices or weekly prices. Daily prices give the most data points so I'll use those.[2]

Second, you look for cyclic content. Chapter 1 discussed used maximum entropy spectral analysis (MESA). Another alternative is Fourier analysis.

Most traders also constrained by how deep their pockets are. The longer the time frame, the greater the excursion of prices and the greater the potential losses they face. Traders who can take the losses from trading daily bars may not be able to handle the swings on a weekly or monthly basis. Some will luxuriate in having the depth to handle a longer time frame while choosing to trade in a shorter time frame, but most traders will intuitively watch the market as much as necessary to control losses in relation to the size of their accounts.

In Chapter 2, all of these considerations, but primarily the cyclic, dictated using averages of 12 and 58 days.

---

[2] I'm also very uneasy with the overnight gaps in prices in intraday data. Try as I have, I cannot find confidence in computations that mix today's five-minute bar with yesterday's.

Ranging

"Trend" is a word that could use some analytical rigor, especially in the trading literature. Frankly, there is a lot less to trading than meets the eye,[3] and the old Dow rule of higher highs, higher lows (or the reverse) is what many trading indicators come down to. At the least, that sort of activity will trigger nearly all indicators looking for trends.

To trade ranges, we're looking for the *absence* of trend within the time frames of 12 and 58 days. Possible rules, among hundreds, include

1. *n*-day range diminishes and volatility declines
2. *n*-day absolute average slope diminishes and volatility declines
3. *not* in trend mode, however trend mode is defined
4. absence of higher highs/higher lows or lower lows/lower highs
5. simple crossing of price over trailing average
6. pivot point highs and lows not exceeded for *n* days

You can see that this speculation could go on forever. Having picked a definition, you'll test it to see if (1) it occurs and (2) it occurs enough for trading. If so, we proceed to trading.

Our Definition

For our purpose of demonstrating campaign tactics, we need only a simple system. We have one in the trend/no trend notion. When the movement of prices kicks us out of our trending state, we have a possible range situation. For the exemplary rules, all that's needed is for one average to go in a different direction from the other. Practically, that's almost always a reversal (a change in direc-

---

[3] A quote often attributed to Richard Dennis. A Chicago speculative trader who's gone boom and bust several times, Dennis is famous for having created a group of trading trainers called the Turtles to prove you could teach trading to others.

tion) of the short average. In Figure 7.3, the prices go from point 1 to point 2 to point 4, rising above the short average at point 3.

One point: During the trend, we record the extremes of price in the trend's direction. That will be one potential side of our range. That's point 2 in Figure 7.3. When persistence in price change and direction (point 1) ends, the averages will go in different directions and we'll be in a nontrending state (point 3).

After we're kicked out of the trend trade, we need to find the reaction level (point 4). Moreover, the reaction level should occur within a reasonable period of time defined by the cyclic periodicity of the tradable. For Crude, we expect that to be within 12 days. After all, if the market is to oscillate back and forth in a range, what more likely time to see cyclic behavior?

Lastly, prices must recross the average to point 5.

What could go wrong here? For one thing, we could never get into a range: we might go right into another trend. Our first hint will be the failure to retrace from point 4 to point 5. Many trends lift off, retrace briefly to retest the area of the previous low, and then resume

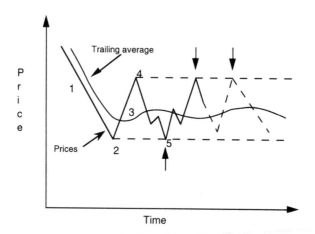

FIGURE 7.3   RANGING MODEL. If the market is not trending, assume it's in a nontrending or ranging market. Although you'll probably never see this idealized situation, an active campaigner will always be alert for the onset of ranging. Once the range is found, the campaigner will trade into the range until forced to reverse into a trend.

their advance. If the trend indicator is working properly, it will kick back into trend mode and the ranging idea will be shelved.

Another bad possibility is that the tradable might not stay in our newly defined range. There's nothing that says a market must trade about a central value or that the value must be constant. All that is just a hypothesis. The worst of these situations is a broadening range, one of which popped up in the 1994 Crude market (see Figure 7.4).

Another thing that can go wrong with range trading is a market that settles on the upper or lower range. What if the market wanders around one of our trading levels, whipsawing back and forth? Will we survive being long (see Figure 7.5) in a slowly falling market? Are there a lot of these situations? Do they make it impossible to trade ranges? Points like these can only be settled by experience, not *a priori*, because we don't know how markets work nor all the factors influencing them at any given time. We must examine the specifics of our experience given defined trading rules and

FIGURE 7.4   BROADENING FORMATION. As highs go higher and lows go lower, range trading becomes impossible without serious losses. This was one of two broadening formations in 11 years.

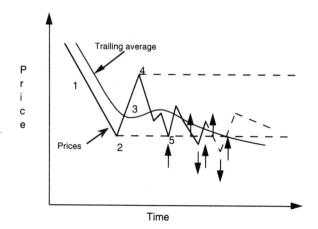

FIGURE 7.5   RANGE WHIPSAW. One thing that may go wrong with trading ranges occurs when prices whipsaw across range lines.

see if the rules generate distinctive distributions of loss for winning trades and losing trades.

RANGE TRADING MAE

Now, we're interested in how far bad a winning range trade goes in Crude. Our game plan is to trade at the range levels into the range and exit when we've crossed to the other side. When we do that, some trades will work, some will be immediate losses and some will be in between, as shown in Figure 7.6.

In Figure 7.6, we trade back into the range at point 6 before giving up and reversing long at point 7. The whole question is where the stop-reverse level is and the only answer is experience. We'll trade in this manner and see what the adverse price movement experience tells us.

Defining Ranges for a Computer

Let's define these situations for a computer and see what it finds. Use the following rules, keeping in mind that they are specific to the example of Crude oil.

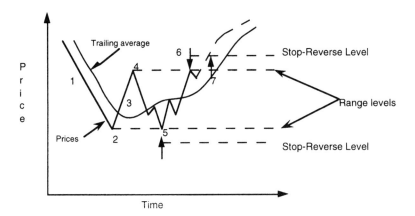

FIGURE 7.6   REVERSING OUT OF RANGE TRADING. Plan on taking a loss when breaking out of your range. Ideally, that will be somewhat offset by the profit going from point 5 to point 6.

1. A trend of at least six days must exist. That is, both averages are moving together for six days. Why six days? As shown in the charts of the trend lengths in Figure 7.7, the genuine trends seem to last longer than five days, at least the trends as we have defined them. Also, six days is the half-cycle length for the short-term average we're using. Because the chart is consistent with cyclic content, I use six days as a good starting point.

2. Trend is broken by prices crossing an average (usually the short average) and forcing it out of sync with its partner. During the trend, we've accumulated the lowest/highest close,[4] which will be our initial guesstimate of one side of the range.

3. Once prices cross the average, we seek the high side of the range as long as trending does not resume. (Again, trending would need to be in evidence for at least six days.) If ranging is in force, the prices should make that reaction high or low and then recross the average,[5] at which point the reaction's

---

[4] Within the last 12 days, that being the cyclic length we're using.

[5] Formally, within 6 days (the half-cycle length) of originally crossing the average. Given the slop in estimates of cyclic length, I give it up to the full cycle length: 12 days.

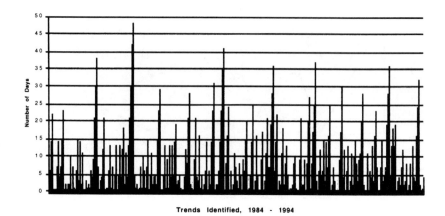

Trends Identified, 1984 - 1994

FIGURE 7.7 DAYS IN TREND. As defined by the two moving averages, trend signals lasting longer than five days have a good chance of solidifying into a strong move. Coming out of trends identified this way will be the setup for identifying a range.

extreme close will be the opposite side of our range (see Figure 7.8).

A choice exists in declaring a range: once when price recrosses and closes across the average after setting a reaction high/low *or* when the price returns to the original low/high set during trending. The former is the more aggressive and is shown in Figure 7.8. If you wait for price to return to the trend high or low (now one side of the range), you'll just have fewer ranges to handle. One way or the other, you must define the retracement from the reaction level in order to define the reaction side of the range.

4. Prices recross the average. A range is declared.

Now we can trade into the range at these two levels with an exit at (1) the opposite side of the range (the hope), (2) after six days of range breakout[6] (the worst result), or (3) when trend is reestablished (that is, ranging is finished).

---

[6] This probably seems arbitrary, and it is. We just need to cut off trades directed into the range when, instead of moving into the range, price breaks out. All such

FIGURE 7.8   ESTABLISHING A RANGE. Prices crossing the trend-defining average define range boundaries at points 2 and 4. Later, as prices decline at point 6, they accord with a declining long average for 12 days, reestablishing a downtrend and forcing an exit from range mode.

As you can see from Figures 7.7–7.9, seemingly simple rules become complex faced with actual market action. Faced with all the weird sequences of prices the market can throw at you, there's the temptation to add other conditions (minimum range size, time in range, minimum changes in the average, volatility above or below certain values, you name it). However, add other conditions sparingly. This example probably has too many cute rules already and, even so, didn't generate enough trades in 11 years to have statistically reliable results.

RESULTS

Looking at the experience trading Crude with these rules generates the graph in Figure 7.10. As usual, the distinction between the ad-

---

trades go into our losers column and generally have huge MAEs. They are also good candidates for reversals.

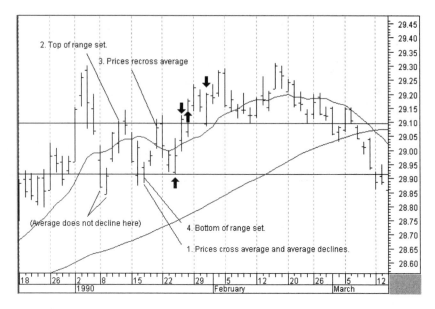

FIGURE 7.9   RANGING EXAMPLE. Carefully note the sequence of decision rules. A classic range, this pricing generates a win across the range, a loser going back into the range and a winner reversing out of the range. Traders' eyes will see a broader range around 29.30—it just wasn't captured by our rules.

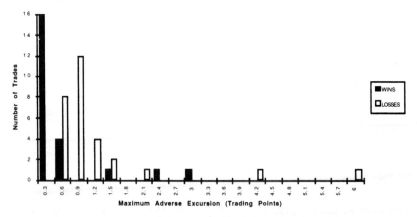

FIGURE 7.10   RANGING MAE. Wins and losses versus MAE, range trading, 1984–1994. Trading into ranges gives distinct distributions of adverse price movement for winners and losers but the "tail" of the winners' distribution is bigger than usual.

verse movement of winners and losers is present, even in this, the fourth mode of trading presented here. The MAEs seem to be generally larger than those seen in the trending mode, too. Finding the stop is not as clear cut as some we've seen, and we need to make a practical choice between a stop at .3 and one at .6, keeping in mind that we're likely to use the point we pick not only as a stop but as a reversal point.

First, let's expand the scale between 0 and .6 to see if some more detail helps. We should be cautious about this: there are not 30 examples of winners or losers in ten years, so the reliability of this estimate is low. Only if there is a perceptibly sharp cutoff will we find anything meaningful. Figure 7.11 shows our findings.

There is nothing easy here. Past .3 there is no sharp cutoff and, moreover, there are relatively few instances in each bin, making any judgment very uncertain. Faced with real-world situations like this, we should take a look at the profitability curve for different cutoff levels: .3, .4, .5, .6, and so on. Figure 7.12 shows the results of the impact of stops.

Again, just as in the real world, we're faced with difficult choices. Given our assumed capital constraint of .6, there are apparently a number of places we could put the stops up to that point. The sharp distinction between .1 and .2 is probably artificial as is the

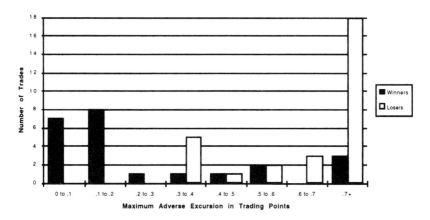

FIGURE 7.11   DETAILED MAE BREAKDOWN. Winners and losers versus MAE, range trading, 1984–1994.

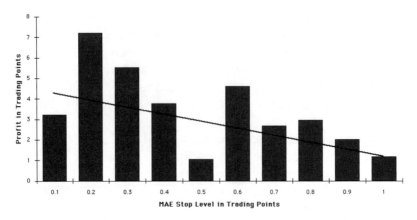

FIGURE 7.12   PROFITABILITY VS. MAE STOPS. Range trading, 1984–1994. Although profitability generally declines as stops are widened, the information is vague given the low number of trades (52).

sharp change between .5 and .6, an artifact of the low number of trades (64). Furthermore, this is just the final distribution of profit versus stop level. Over time, that distribution changed quite a bit, as seen in Figures 7.13 and 7.14.

As a result, making an operating decision comes down to the analyst's art, restricted by the capital constraints. Looking at the final profitability (Figure 7.12) after 11 years of experience and keeping in mind the variability just discussed, I've eyeballed a steadily downward sloping line from left to right, ignoring the peaks and valleys. Given that approximation, I don't see a clean cutoff from this data. Because we've used .3 for all our trading examples to date and though there's no reason this set of rules couldn't have another level, .3 is a reasonable choice here as well. It's also the level that lets us double our contracts within our capital constraints. It's the one I'll use for this campaign.

Descriptive Behavior

Analyzing markets from the point of entry of a specific set of trading rules is usually only done for profitability purposes. It can also

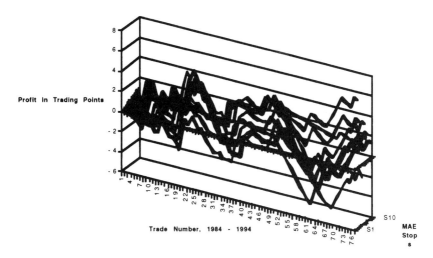

FIGURE 7.13   PROFIT OVER TIME. Cumulative profitability, reversing out of ranges, 1984–1994. I plotted profitability for various MAE stops over time. Although the detail is impossible to read, the message is that (1) profitability increases over time and (2) profitability is extremely variable. Figure 7.12 shows the final points end-on.

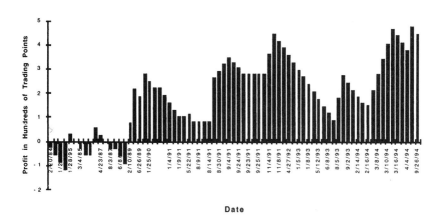

FIGURE 7.14   RANGE TRADING AT .3 STOP LEVEL. Profit or loss, 1984–1994. To provide more detail than the graphs above, this chart shows the equity line when the MAE stop level is set just above .3. Although the trend is upward, notice the strong variability.

be interesting and profitable simply to learn of typical market behavior. That there might exist "typical" market behavior is contro-
versial, and I certainly don't have proof that anything like it exists,
just observations.

Crude's trading ranges were defined by the rules earlier in the
chapter, and anyone else could come up with other rules. It still
struck me that range sizes were generally consistent. If you graph
frequency versus range size, you don't come up with a random
smear. Instead you get the distribution shown in Figure 7.15. In
this graph, the outliers[7] are for a wild series of trades around the
1990–1991 New Year as the market reacted to having reached the
astounding price of $40 a barrel for oil that had a marginal cost of
$3–$5. This series of trades met the definition of a trading range,
and the results must be included in the analysis. Trading today, I'd
be inclined to ignore them if today's prices were ranging 200–400
points per day.

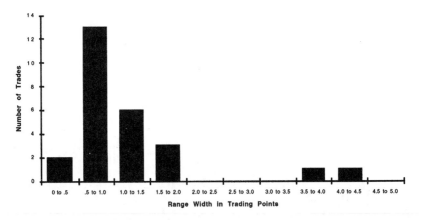

FIGURE 7.15   TRADING RANGES. Range width, 1984–1994. Crude
trading ranges are about 100 trading points wide, unadjusted for
volatility. This observation gives the trader some targets when he or she
is fading a reaction or calling the limits of a range.

---

[7] An *outlier* is a data point noticeably far from the bulk of the data, in this case
range widths of 300 to 400 trading points.

The rest of the ranges were clustered between .43 and 1.8, which may seem an unmanageable range. That depends on the depth of your pockets. At least it gives you some idea of where to start probing reactions that may turn into ranges. There aren't enough of these situations to generate good observations, let alone good statistics, so for now, fading a reaction repeatedly until you end up entering at the right level can't be more rigorously defined.

Breakouts

Another characteristic of Crude ranges that caught my eye was the frequency with which they broke out in continuations of their long-term (12–week) trend (see Figure 7.16). Using these trading rules, the initial extreme was the low or high for the trend (point 2); the reaction defining the range went to a reaction high or low (point 4); and you trade the range when prices recross the average and then return to the initial extreme low or high (point 5)—at which point you find yourself trading against the long-term trend.

In 18 out of 26 cases, trading into the range at point 5 resulted in an immediate loss that reversed into a trend trade. Eighteen of the

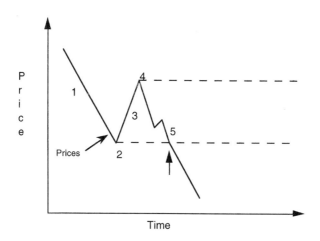

FIGURE 7.16   BREAKING OUT OF RANGES.

12 trades had *no* favorable price movement at all. That is, they broke through the range very sharply, making implementation of stops difficult. This may be a point at which using an option would be better than a stop, a topic explored in Chapter 10.

To me, this behavior is an evocation of the concepts of "support" and "resistance," as well as the idea of breaking through either one. Evidently, in Crude oil, these levels can be roughly defined by ranging rules, and breaking through them can serve as a guide for trend direction. So dramatic is this effect that it forms the basis for Chapter 8.

Duration of Ranges

It won't surprise Crude oil traders, I suppose, to find that trading ranges didn't last long (see Figure 7.17). Of the 26 trading ranges, only 10 lasted long enough for more than 1 trade and only 4 lasted long enough for 4 trades. From entry to exit ranged from 18 to 73 days, and most (12 of 26) were 20 to 30 days long, this after taking 6 to 12 days to get into and define a range. I know of no reason trading ranges should be of any specific length but I now suspect that any Crude ranges over 30 days are long of tooth.

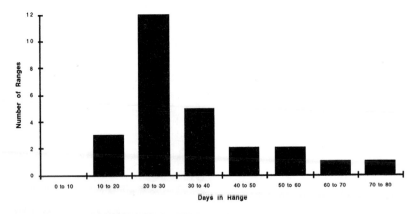

FIGURE 7.17   DAYS IN RANGE.

SUMMARY

One idea that doesn't work out in Crude as well as hoped is that the small loss taken on breaking out would be offset by profits from trending across the range. Whereas some ranges (1) last long enough and (2) have the extremes revisited by prices, more often, once the range is defined, prices tend toward the side of their eventual breakout. On a chart, you get a triangle toward the breakout side rather than an even oscillation across the range.

Losses from trading into a range in a strongly trending market like Crude oil can be quite dramatic because your first trade may be against the trend. This emphasizes the importance of proper loss control. Nevertheless, defining ranges roughly and trading into them did produce profits with limited risk of disaster.

Win size was limited by the automatic exit at the opposite side of the trading range whereas losing trades were terminated on the sixth day after entry or on the sixth day of a new long-term and short-term trend. The effect was to heighten losses and limit profitability. Indeed, range trading is probably only feasible with MAE stops. Without them, wins are limited and losses could be huge. Table 7.1 shows the 1984–1994 profitability for New York Light Crude.

TABLE 7.1   CAMPAIGN TRADING PROFITABILITY NEW YORK LIGHT CRUDE, 1984–1994

Mode	Rule	Stop Level	Profit/Loss (points)
Trend	Two moving average	.31	3,600
Trend	Add-on day-trades	.31	2,500
Trend	Add-on position trades	.31	640
Trend	Reversal	.31	1,827
Range	Trade into range	.31	550

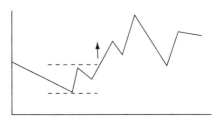

8
Reversing Out of Ranges

By now, a campaign trader will have a full plate. Although the different phases of the campaign tend to take place sequentially, the constant alternation from trending to nontrending with its overlapping trades keeps you busy tracking a variety of positions with a variety of stops and margin requirements. We're still not finished developing the campaign, though.

In Chapter 7 the idea of trading into trading ranges was discussed with the result that (1) we could practically identify ranges and (2) we could trade into them with specific distributions of adverse price movement for both winning and losing trades. Those results let us stop out our range trades at .31 or $310 of risk on a single-contract basis.

Recall now that when trend trading was discussed, the idea came up that an MAE stop level might be a good reversal point. The idea was that, if good trades don't hit the MAE stop, a trade that does hit the MAE stop must be a 'bad' trade that could be converted to a 'good' trade if it were reversed. Of course, not all trades that hit the MAE stop are destined to be losers, but as it happened, reversing bad trend trades at the MAE stop level was profitable.

Now it's time to see if the same thing applies to range trades. After all, ranges are just another form of trend—persistently, consistently flat. Plus, a trade that hits the MAE stop is most likely 'bad.'

The tough part here is that Figure 7.10 shows that, when range trading, more winning trades than usual have large adverse excursions. If a range trade is bad, there's a possibility that reversing at that point would make a good trade, especially since our underlying hypothesis is that a breakout of the range must occur with a loss on the range trade before getting into trending. Thus a reversal of the 'bad' range trade would get us right with a new trend right out of the blocks. Figure 8.1 is a reprise of a previous figure explaining this idea.

REALITY

Does this sort of thing ever really happen? Even if it does, how can an abstract number like .31 be the 'magic' turnaround point? Figure 8.2 shows an exemplary reverse trade, and Figure 8.3 shows a disastrous reversal.

Surprisingly, good things happen fairly often. Seen in the light of ranges defined by moving averages, not only do ranges occur fairly

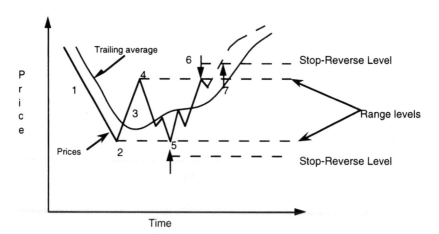

FIGURE 8.1   REVERSING OUT OF RANGE TRADING. Plan on taking a loss when breaking out of your range. Ideally, that will be somewhat offset by the profit going from point five to point six.

FIGURE 8.2   EXEMPLARY REVERSE TRADE. Crude breaks out of a trading range for a sharp 200–point drop. Reversing out of a trading range is a relatively high-percentage trade in Crude, but the MAE stops are wider than in other types of trades.

often in Crude, but breaking out of them by as much as .31 tends to presage trending and sharp profitability. Only 5 of the 38 reversing trades had no favorable movement at all after being put on .31 outside the range. Of the trades that reversed out of a range, 30 (whether eventual winners or losers) lasted more than five days, as shown in Figure 8.4.

This may be tradable information: it gives one time to put in trailing exits to minimize losses. In contrast are trading rules generating trades that, if they go sour, do so quickly. As it happens, reversing Crude trades don't tend to go to pot rapidly. These trades persist, and 33 of 35 had at least some favorable excursion. Slightly less than half had a favorable excursion greater than the range from which they originated, so there's some momentum coming out of a range (see Figure 8.5).

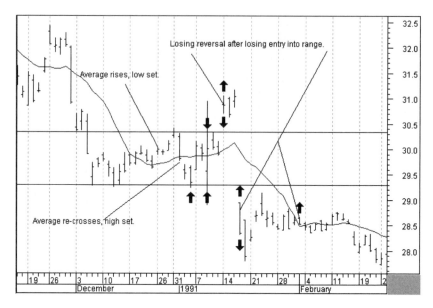

FIGURE 8.3   A DISASTROUS REVERSAL. Although this range met the mechanical criteria, price action made reversing out of it—at both top and bottom—an expensive disaster.

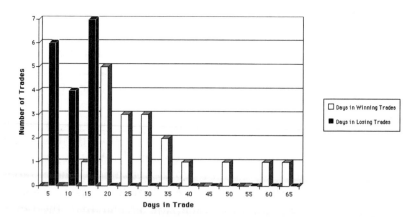

FIGURE 8.4   DAYS IN TRADE. Of course, winning reversals lasted longer than losers, but note that even losers often lasted more than five days before succumbing.

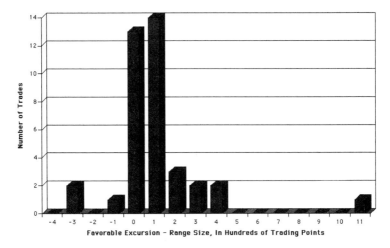

FIGURE 8.5   FAVORABLE EXCURSION. Although it's unlikely a relationship could be quantified, reversals out of ranges in Crude tend to be about the size of the range from which they came, or somewhat larger.

God forbid anyone would use this information for targeting a price level on the breakout from a range, but it is striking that upon breakout you can expect favorable movement about the size of the previous range, with some tendency toward exceeding the range size. Although this could not be put into rigid trading rules without many more examples to generate statistical confidence, it is enough to get my attention. Perhaps price excursion, seen relative to its own prior behavior, may be somewhat ordered. Consider how unlikely it should be that there exists any relationship between breakout price movement, both long and short, and a range arbitrarily defined by prices moving about an arbitrary average over 11 years of widely varying market movements, yet Figures 8.5 and 8.6 suggests just that.[1]

That Crude trades off support and resistance levels and around value points probably isn't a surprise to oil traders, and here's concrete evidence of it.

---

[1] Curiosities like this are benefits of studying price behavior in terms of excursion from points defined by trading rules.

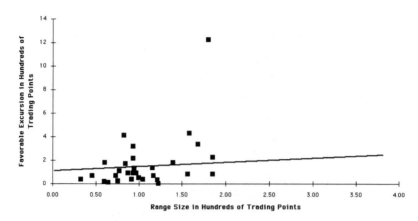

FIGURE 8.6   FAVORABLE EXCURSION VS. RANGE SIZE. Reversing out of ranges. Another way of looking at the same data as in Figure 8.5, the linear estimate of the relationship between range size and excursion shows great variability. Note the clustering of range size about 100 ($1.00 per barrel) trading points.

Why .31 as the stop/reversal point? I hope it's evident that .31 isn't something logically derived from theory but an estimate made from the recorded experience of the market's own behavior. Had I used different rules to define a range, a different set of distributions would have been generated and .31 might have become 1.07 or some other number.

Each trader sees the market through the prism of his own rules and, from that perception, generates his own experience, which the MAE technique records. Hopefully, the results are operational, but it's very possible that the rules don't discern between winning and losing trades. Then, not only would the number not be .31, it would not exist at all; there would be no evident point at which stops should be placed.

RESULTS

To speak specifically, reversing defined range trades at .31 generated 35 trades, of which 19 were winners (see Figure 8.7).

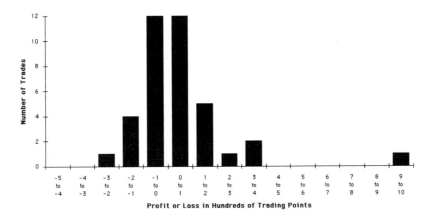

FIGURE 8.7   REVERSING PROFIT DISTRIBUTION. In contrast to trend trading where only one trade in three was profitable, reversing is about a 50–50 proposition before stops.

There may be a slight skew[2] to this distribution given its single huge winner, but its symmetry impresses me most. I had the impression when going through the trades that the winners were far larger than the losers so I also estimated the profitability for each of these bins. Without stops, just plain reversing out of trading ranges at .31 generated the distribution of profitability shown in Figure 8.8.

It turned out that my impression wasn't accurate. The winners were more profitable than the losers (by 1,350 points) but not hugely so if the single large win is discounted. Losers were more concentrated in just three bins while winners spread out more to the upside. I forbear giving the sums of profits and losses in favor of your inspecting the chart's shape for information on the tendencies of this trading rule.

These figures show that even if there is no effort to minimize losses, reversing out of a range is a good idea in trading Crude. The next question is always, "Should we use stops and, if so, where?"

---

[2] For those familiar with these numbers, the skew of this distribution is 2.7, kurtosis 11.6.

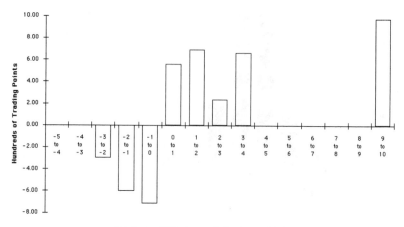

Categories of Wins/Losses in Hundreds of Trading Points

FIGURE 8.8   TOTAL PROFIT/LOSS VS. SIZE OF WIN/LOSS.
Converting Figure 8.7 to profit or loss in trading points, the distribution
shows a slight advantage to the winners, even ignoring the single huge
win to the far right.

As usual by now, the first thing to look at is the adverse price
movement that trades reversing out of a trading range experience.

Looking at the familiar pattern in Figure 8.9, we see that in reversing out of a range, winning trades just don't go very far against
you. The graph doesn't give much detail between .3 (the level we've
used elsewhere for a stop) and .6 (our capital constraint), so we
need to elaborate the information and ask what happens to profitability as stops run from .3 on up. Figure 8.10 shows what we find.

Interpreting this chart, I'm struck by the consistent rise and fall
of the values. Not that the news is great: it looks as though my fa-
vorite stop, .31, is not close to the optimum. Somewhere around .5
is a maximum surrounded by other high levels of profitability.

Given the variability in profit seen in the last chapter (Figure
7.13), we should check it here. Looking at the cumulative profitability over time, not only do stops increase profitability, they reduce
the variability of the results dramatically, as shown in Figure 8.11.

Here, again, an analyst's art will be in picking the right cutoff
point for his or her program. Personally, not trusting these values
as being too explicit (only 35 trades in 11 years), I'd use an MAE

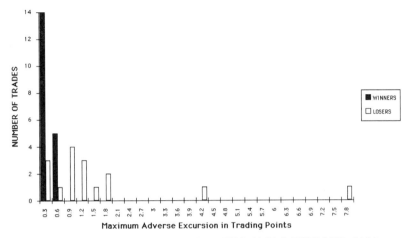

FIGURE 8.9   REVERSING MAE. WINNERS AND LOSERS VS. MAE.
Reversing out of a range shows that adverse movement can be
horrendous (as in 1990–1991) but is generally concentrated in the first
six bins while winning trades don't go more than $600 against you.

stop of .5, comfortably into the profitable range and also comfortably below my capital cutoff point. Others might cut things
finely at .4, taking most of the additional profit and the smallest
additional losses. Others might get farther into the profitable

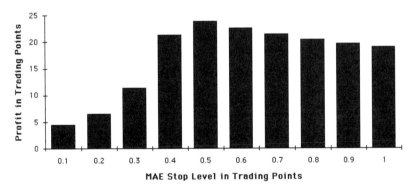

FIGURE 8.10   PROFIT VS. MAE ON REVERSING. As stops are raised
from .1 up, the significant jump in overall profits is between .3 and .4,
an extra $100 of loss per contract offset by overall profits rising from
1,100 points to 2,130 points.

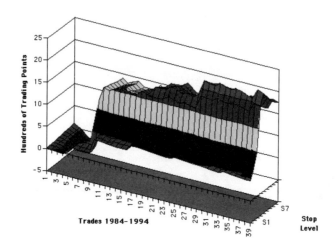

FIGURE 8.11   CUMULATIVE PROFITABILITY. Reversing becomes more steadily profitable, with less variability, when MAE stops are used. Figure 8.10 reversing looks at this shape end-on.

range with .6 or .7, but beyond that we may be looking at huge, uncontrollable excursions (gaps in pricing) that aren't worth the exposure.

Taking .5 as the cutoff for reversal trades out of a range generates a net trading profit of 2,229 trading points.

Trade Behavior

I enjoyed analyzing reversal trades in Crude. The contract often breaks cleanly through support and resistance, at least as it's defined here, and goes on to trending. As a result, often before the trend trading starts, you're already on-board the trend.

It's worth noting that the reversal trade shouldn't be 'converted' to a trend trade once things are going well; it has its own separate capitalization and loss level (.51) that is different from that of the trend trade (.31). Trending trades will kick off with their own signals and loss levels when both averages start moving in the same direction.

SUMMARY

In the previous chapter, our campaigning trader was simply looking for a way to extract some capital from a trendless market. It was good news that an MAE stop could be defined for a trading range, as well as for a trending activity. It turned out that, without MAE, stops would have been quite tough to set and trading the range problematic. With MAE stops, range trading was feasible but not hugely profitable.

In this chapter, pushing our luck further, we were able to define MAE stops for reversing out of the range as well, giving us another source of profit. It turned out that for the first time in this analysis, the MAE was greater than the .31 we'd used in all the previous trading rules as shown in Table 8.1. As a further result, with a capital constraint of $600 or so, we'd only be able to trade one contract using these rules unless we're willing to accept a much lower estimated profitability.

From a campaigner's point of view, reversing out of a trading range in Crude is a vital tactic. On average, three of these ranges will crop up every year, and once their levels are broken, there is a strong possibility of a strong move. The profitability level isn't as big as trend trading but it's right up there with add-on trading, building a trader's strength and trading capacity. It kicks one into the same direction as trend trading, too, perhaps earlier if everything goes exactly right, so it's psychologically advantageous as well.

**TABLE 8.1 CAMPAIGN TRADING PROFITABILITY
NEW YORK LIGHT CRUDE, 1984–1994**

Mode	Rule	Stop Level	Profit/Loss (points)
Trend	Two moving averages	.31	3,600
Trend	Add-on day-trades	.31	2,500
Trend	Add-on position trades	.31	640
Trend	Reversal	.31	1,827
Range	Trade into range	.31	550
Range	Reverse out of range	.51	2,229

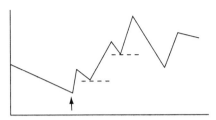

9

Minimum Favorable Excursion

HOW LITTLE DO TRADES GO OUR WAY?

If it is worth knowing how bad things get during a trade, what about looking at how good they get? Maximum adverse excursion measures how far against us both winners and losers go. What's the *least* we can count on winners and losers going *for* us?

For purposes of analysis, let's again split things into the performances of winners and losers. For each category, we want to know the maximum amount the trade went for us before ending. Even before looking at the results, we'd expect that losers wouldn't show much movement in our favor and that winners would. We already know that winners don't go very far against us and that losers do. Again, we won't check chart formations, averages, indicators, or anything but the actual excursion of prices from the point of entry.

Protective Stops

Over the years, authors Edward Gotthelf, Tushar Chande, and myself have explored how favorably trades move eventually, looking for guidelines to managing trades in place.[1] This was usually to find good exits. I'd settle for something less at this juncture: a good place to raise our stops from the MAE point, preferably without giving up profits prematurely.

Even to achieve breakeven on a good number of losers would be a major achievement because it could alter the ratio of wins and losses from 30:70 to, say, 50:50, increasing profitability in the process.

Reversing trades in Crude are a good example to use for this because, from Chapter 8, we have graphic evidence that reversals out of ranges have a good percentage of winners and tend to go one trading range or more to the upside when they succeed. That is, when they win, they go somewhere. How far do they go, and do they go for enough to let us put a stop below the trade at some point, rationally cutting off winning trades that turn into losers late in life?

What would the impact be if a stop were placed at, say, breakeven once a trade had advanced as much as .3 or .6 or .9? In other words, can we profitably cut off the loss we're going to take from trades that are to become losers or will we cut off too many eventual winners?

Favorable Price Excursion

Figure 9.1 shows the basic picture. Initially, prices advance (whether we're long or short) favorably. At some favorable excursion, we're encouraged to move our stop up from the MAE level. How far do we move it? Of course, good ideas can go bad, as demonstrated in Figure 9.2.

---

[1] Edward B. Gotthelf, *The Commodex System* (New York: Commodex Systems Corp., 1974), pg. 90 (originally published in 1959); Tushar Chande and Stanley Kroll, *The New Technical Trader* (New York: John Wiley & Sons, Inc., 1994); John Sweeney, presentation at TAG Conference, Las Vegas, Nev., 1994; also John Sweeney, "Settlement," in *Technical Analysis of Stocks and Commodities* (Seattle: 1991, 1992), November 1991–September 1992.

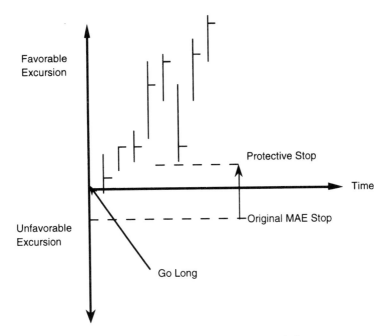

FIGURE 9.1   MOVING UP STOPS. In this idealized diagram, measured from entry, the trade initially goes in our favor but later retreats. Where should the protective stop be placed, if used at all?

Figures 9.1 and 9.2 are idealized, but should get the idea across. If we have a winner we'd move the stop up along with the advancing prices. Familiar methods for doing this include using trend lines, parabolic stops, dynamic moving averages, previous resistance levels, and others. These methods are usually oriented toward exiting a trade at the end of a trend. Here, again, I'm looking for something more limited: to prevent an initially favorable advance from turning into a loss.

The Best Yardstick?

What is the best measure of favorable excursion? Can we judge from how favorably the trade has gone when to move up the stop

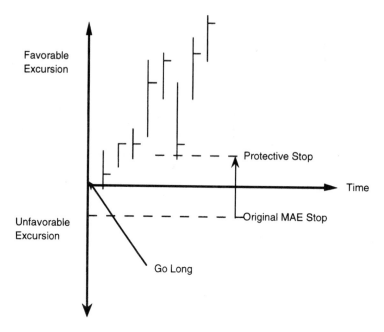

FIGURE 9.2   HITTING THE STOP. Naturally, if things can go well, they can go poorly. Here, the protective stop knocks out a much greater profit.

to breakeven? If so, how far is far enough? That is, given favorable movement *x*, what is *y* for stop placement?

In this situation, the price closest to the proposed protective stop isn't the *maximum favorable excursion* (MaxFE) (Figure 9.3), but the *minimum favorable excursion* (the distance to the highest low in an advance or the lowest high in a decline). Before going further, let me define minimum favorable excursion (MinFE) by example.

Why use the nearest low if long or the nearest high if short? These are the best proxies for the chance of a protective stop being hit. In Figure 9.4, an example taken from action in 1984 Crude, the reversal trade was made during the first bar, going long. The maximum favorable excursion for the next ten days was hit that same day. The trade ended a winner on the last bar shown.

If we wanted to know where to set a protective stop, the first day is no help at all because the low was below the stop and the high

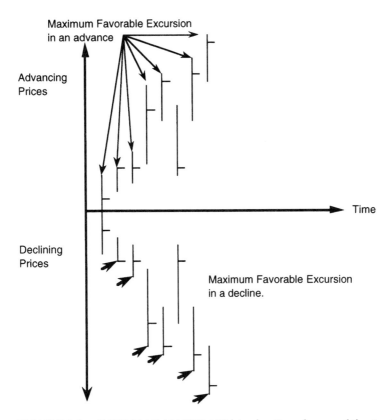

FIGURE 9.3   DEFINING MAXFE. Within the time frame of the trade, MaxFE is the distance from the entry to the highest high in a long position or the lowest low in a short position.

gave no clue. On the next two days, the lows were below the entry level and the highs, though above entry level, were below the maximum favorable excursion. If we had tried to estimate the likely stop level, MaxFE would not have helped.

It wasn't until the fourth day that there was any space at all between the entry level and the low of the day. Still, the fourth day was a more reasonable place to think of moving up a stop rather than the first couple of days. Lows act as a conservative minimum distance from the point of entry (when going long) even though there is still a role for the maximum favorable excursion.

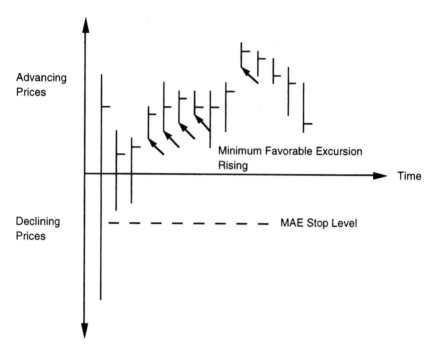

FIGURE 9.4   MEASURING FAVORABLE EXCURSION. From the point of entry in a purchase, minimum favorable excursion is the difference between the highest low encountered and the entry price with a minimum of zero.

In the first place, there's necessarily a strong relation between the two, as shown in Figure 9.5. However, the interesting situations are the eight times (clustered on the Y axis) when the MinFE was zero and the MaxFE was positive. In all these cases, the reversal was a loser but the price jump outside the range boundaries triggered the reversal. In terms of going long, the high established a MaxFE, but the lows, if there was more than one day to the trade, never went above entry. There are far too few cases to establish any rules, but this occurrence raises the question of which would be the better proxy for moving stops, especially when the MinFE is zero.

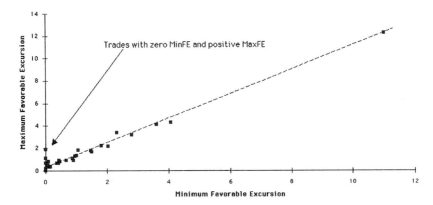

FIGURE 9.5   BAD TRADES GOING GOOD. MinFE and MaxFE are strongly related (they are opposite ends of the same price bar) except in cases where there is no minimum favorable excursion.

FINDING WINNERS AND MINIMIZING LOSERS

Is there an edge we can find here? Is there a point of favorable excursion that, once reached, creates the fair likelihood that a protective stop won't be picked? Let's look at the exemplary information for reversal trades.

Figure 9.6 shows a distinct difference between the minimum favorable excursions of winners and losers. The losers' minimum favorable excursions are usually less than .3. Only 1 in 16 is more than .3. As expected, favorable excursions trail off to the right, and as hoped for, there is relatively little overlap between the two distributions because only three winners had MinFE of less than .6, whereas all the losers were bunched.

In other words, just as winning trades don't go very far against us, losing trades don't go very far in our favor *if we measure by MinFE.*

What about maximum favorable excursions (MaxFE)? Given the close relationship with MinFE, wouldn't MaxFE serve just as well? Also, if we used MaxFE, could we get some guidance about those eight trades with a positive MaxFE and no MinFE? Figure 9.7 shows the distribution.

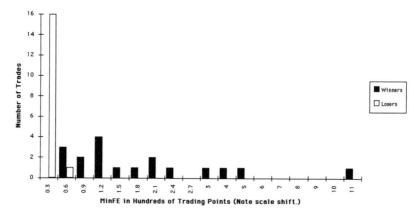

FIGURE 9.6   SHARP DISTINCTION. Minimum favorable excursion produces clearly different distributions for winning trades and losing trades. When reversing out of a range, a trade with a MinFE of more than .3 is highly likely to be a winner.

This is a muddier picture. There is a lot of overlap between these two distributions. One of the losers had a maximum favorable excursion of around 2.1. Yet these trades are the same as those in the previous figure. MinFE provides a sharp distinction between even-

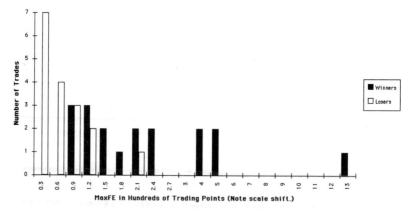

FIGURE 9.7   OVERLAPPING DISTRIBUTIONS. Measuring favorable excursion using maximum favorable excursion makes distinguishing winners and losers tough.

tual winners and eventual losers while MaxFE does not, at least using these rules with Crude.

So, as a first cut, we'd use MinFE and look for a reversing trade with a MinFE > .3 (or .6 to cover all the bases). There'd be no need to move up the stop protectively in this case because our experience (see Figure 9.6) indicates that this trade is likely to be a winner and we don't want to put that at risk with a closer stop.[2]

Of course, on the downside, if the reversing trade instead hit our MAE stop, our trade management problem would be over: we'd be out of the trade. It's the gray area in between—where the trade has not been stopped out or advanced more than MinFE > .3—that a protective stop may have its place.

GRAY AREAS

Do losing reversal trades give us a chance to get out whole or at least with less of a loss than the MAE stop? In other words, what is the distribution of the movement of losing trades in our favor? For example, in Figure 9.7, there was one trade that was 2.1 points in our favor at one time. To have that turn into a loss is very damaging.

As it turns out, there is some opportunity on virtually every trade when we look at MaxFE (see Figure 9.8). All but one losing trade had some favorable excursion, potentially giving us some room to move up a protective stop. This is not the case with MinFE, as shown in Figure 9.9. With MinFE, some losing trades had no minimum favorable excursion at all, indicating that there was no room to move up a stop.

I'm particularly interested in the trades with MinFE < .3—a range that includes those with none or zero MinFE—and/or trades with MaxFE > 0. From Figure 9.6, these trades are suspect: until they achieve MinFE > .3, they could be losers, which will cost us the MAE stop. Just eyeballing Figure 9.9, we can see that most are likely losers. Can we cut them off early?

---

[2] Especially because breakouts often lead to trends, we may start thinking of add-on trades for the reversal. These would be taken along the lines described in Chapter 5.

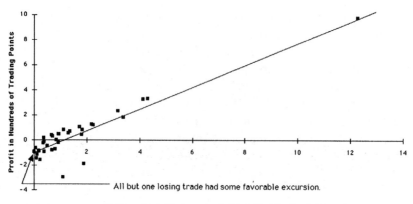

FIGURE 9.8   SOME FAVORABLE MOVEMENT. It turns out that even losing trades have some favorable movement. The question is where to cut it off without damaging winning trades.

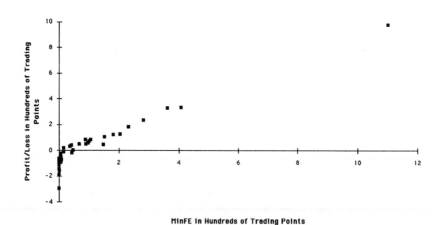

FIGURE 9.9   LESS FAVORABLE MOVEMENT. Minimum favorable excursion gives a sharper cutoff between winners and losers but less room to move up a protective stop.

To look at the gray area more closely, let's plot MaxFE and MinFE for trades where MinFE < .3 and MaxFE > 0. In Figure 9.10 every trade with a MinFE below .3 was a loser. It even turns out that my .3 definition of a bin was coarse: .16 would have done, though that's vague given the sparseness of the data. Still, it's tantalizing that even .1 would have gotten all but two of these losing trades. It holds the promise that a trade with a MinFE > .1 could be allowed to run confidently while those less than .1 could be cut off early on.

Unfortunately, Figure 9.10 shows no neat cutoff point, only information for the trader to consider. Figure 9.11 shows that most of these losers—reversal trades with some maximum favorable excursion—will likely get stopped by the MAE stop. After all, only three of them didn't go below the MAE stop. That indicates, though not conclusively, that the gray area is a very small part of our trading problem: 3 of 35 trades. Moreover, if a trade doesn't hit the stop, it's going to cost us less than the stop, which is something we can bear.

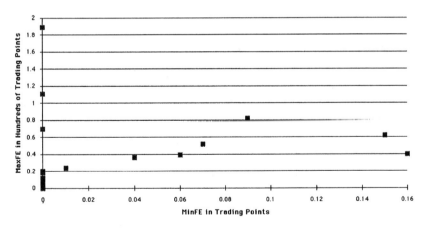

FIGURE 9.10   LOSERS ALL. MinFE versus MaxFE for MinFE < .3. Looking at trades with MinFE less than .3, we find all were losers. Tantalizingly, these 15 trades, nearly half of our experience, indicate that losing trades rarely have MinFE > .16 or even .1.

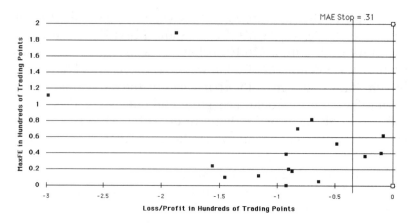

FIGURE 9.11   LOSERS HIT STOPS. Though some go well into the black, there appears no neat point at which trades with low MinFE and positive MaxFE can be cut off.

It turns out in Crude that, when reversing, experience does not suggest a neat point to move up the protective stop. Keep in mind that in these gray-area trades the MinFE does not go more than .3 above the entry (and half the time doesn't even get that far!) while the MaxFE does move strongly in a favorable direction. You have a situation with very long bars. So, if you experience a high MaxFE but the low doesn't rise enough to generate a MinFE greater than .3 (or .1 if you're pressing your luck), you don't have a clear-cut call to raise the protective stop.

If you'd settle for a less clear-cut call, an artful call, I'd suggest moving up the stop to breakeven if MaxFE > .3, even though MinFE < .3, as shown in Figure 9.12. Although .3 seems to keep coming up, the graph itself suggests this level. Around .4 there is an accumulation of MaxFEs, so, though the information is sparse, there's the potential to take advantage. In effect, the rule is that if the trade goes up as much as .3 while the low (in a long trade) never gets above .3 (or .16 to really push things), it'll be closed out when it returns to breakeven. Although there aren't enough of

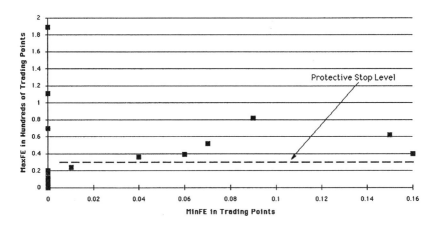

FIGURE 9.12   PROTECTIVE STOP AT .3. Reversal trades with MaxFE > .3 (but MinFE < .3) can be cut off early on with a stop at .3 over entry. This may put the occasional winner with a low MinFE at risk, though that didn't happen in this period.

these situations to justify statistics, inspection shows this worked out favorably in all nine cases, reducing losses that would otherwise have been taken.

FAVORABLE EXCURSION

When things go badly, we stop out, but what about when things go well? Favorable price excursion has its behavioral characteristics as we've just explored, and before leaving the subject I'd like to point out a few more using the reversal trades as examples. I haven't found hard and fast rules using this information, so I present it as additional information you can accumulate to know your tradeable more thoroughly. The "looks" I'll show here could have been assembled for any of the trading modes outlined previously. I have forborne because the campaigner will not get a firm trading rule from it.

Time of Trade

Winning trades very commonly persist long enough to generate profits, and losing trades go downhill quickly. The advantage to this behavior is that you quickly learn if your opinion is wrong and have the opportunity to reverse as we've already discussed. Another advantage: if you take out insurance by using options, you won't burn up much time premium in the four to ten days you need coverage.

Taking a look at reversal trades, how long did winners persist and losers survive?

As shown in Figure 9.13, winners generally last 20 days or more, which reflects the trending that occurs on breakout from a trading range. This persistence gives the breakout its status as a strong indicator of trending activity.

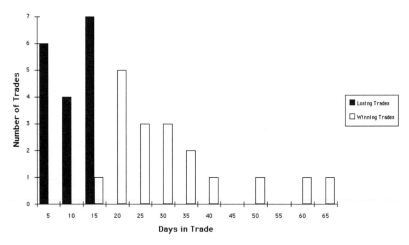

FIGURE 9.13 DAYS IN TRADE. Winning and losing reversal trades. Winners, not surprisingly, last longer than losers when reversing from a trading range. Unusual here is the fair number of losers that last up to 15 calendar days. (Days shown are calendar days, not trading days.)

Normal Advance or Decline

It's more practical to look at *how* winners advance and losers struggle along. Although each trade is unique, looking at the trades graphically from the point of entry makes it possible to see some commonality. Starting with losers, how do they look day to day? Figure 9.14 shows losing reversal trades seen from the point of entry.

Looking at Figure 9.14 puts a picture to the old traders' admonition that if it's not going your way, get out. Without this sort of picture, you always have hope that things will eventually go your way. With this picture, your trade's fate may more probably be seen.

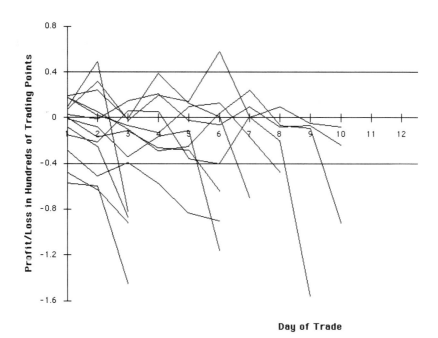

FIGURE 9.14   LOSERS' DAILY GAIN OR LOSS. Not only do reversals out of ranges not go too far for us (on a closing basis), they take their time about doing it. Crude range reversals that end up losers may take up to ten days.

Two things strike me about Figure 9.14. First, nearly all the excursion is between .4 to –.4, implying that not only do losing Crude range reversals not go too far for us but also they don't go too far against us *until the last*. Thinking in terms of a long breakout (a reversal upward out of a range), one that doesn't succeed doesn't seem to reverse sharply back into the range immediately. Second, they take their time about it, meandering about the reversal level (which here was .3 above the range) for up to ten days. This adds to the picture of Crude as a tradable that respects support and resistance because it appears that breaking out of the range by .3 either holds around that breakout level or moves upward sharply, but doesn't immediately or randomly move back into the range. Simply, a reversal out of a range is a relatively safe trade.

Figure 9.15 shows reversal winners. One extraordinary sequence distorts the information on the rest so, deleting that, we get Figure 9.16.

I have eyeballed a channel of advance in Figure 9.16 to highlight the general area that reversals out of ranges generally take. It's always caught my eye that, long or short: 1984 or 1994; high volatil-

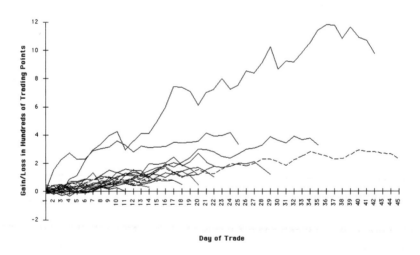

FIGURE 9.15   REVERSAL WINNERS' PROFIT BY DAY. Winning trades naturally last longer than losers and generally cluster along similar lines of advance under all the various conditions of 11 years of trading.

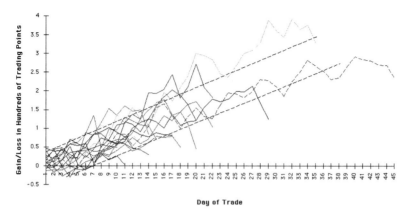

Day of Trade

FIGURE 9.16   REVERSALS WITHOUT OUTLIERS. Omitting two trades that advanced very sharply shows the remainder in better detail. The bulk of the excursion proceeds along a relatively consistent pathway.

ity or low; bonds, futures, or stocks; there is usually some consistency in the market behavior when measured from the point of trading entry, and I see it again here.

Last, for easier comparison with the losers, see Figure 9.17.

There could hardly be a greater contrast in the behavior of winners and losers than in Figures 9.17 and 9.14.[3] For the trader who is psychologically unsure the middle of a trade, looking at these charts and comparing them to the trade he or she is in, can usually help to sort out the situation in a hurry.

I can't reduce the practical effect of these observations to a rule. First, the idea of moving up stops, particularly on winning trades during the first ten days, puts winners at risk:[4] winners may still be flogging about the entry level during that period and could be prematurely cut off. After eight to ten days, they could be reasonably moved up along the lower channel of Figure 9.17, or just to breakeven to be more conservative.

---

[3] Keep in mind that the days shown in these charts are trading days, not calendar days. The days-in-trade numbers in Figure 9.13 are calendar days. This distinction is a programming convenience rather than an analytical necessity.

[4] For these rules trading Crude. It needn't always be this result.

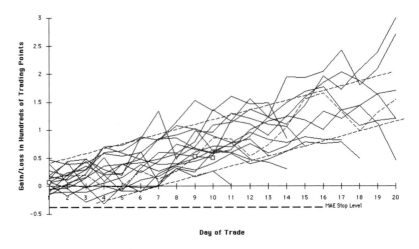

FIGURE 9.17   CLOSE UP: WINNERS BY DAY. Winners in contrast to losers, rarely spend much time in the minus column. Although they do wallow around the +.4 area losers visit, they steadily move upward.

Second, campaigners will not sell their positions at the top of the channel and they'll be reluctant to buy more positions at the bottom. Arbitrarily adding positions as the trade advances in between the upper and lower boundaries can be achieved as described in earlier chapters. Perhaps when doing so it's enough to see the underlying reversal trade in question is proceeding according to form—or not. For example, an add-on trade when the underlying reversal trade is on the bottom of the channel might be forgone. I've never tested this logic, but having read eight chapters of my methods, you can well imagine how I'd go about it.

CAMPAIGNING

By now the typical trader has his or her hands full monitoring market modes, trading tactics, trading situations, and capital requirements for several different regimens in just one tradable. If you multiply this by tens or hundreds of tradables, the need for automation of trading is clear.

Even more essential is continuing to grasp the overall point of the program: equity growth. For that, portfolio management software is essential as each new opportunity will be taken with reference to total capital available. The campaigner may include open equity in that figure, but the conservative will not. The more conservative would include only the negative open equity.

Moving Up Stops

This chapter looked at using favorable excursion to find a place to move up stops. It turned out that there were few opportunities to do this in Crude.[5] If a trade went south, it took out the MAE stop pretty quickly. If it went north decisively, as measured by MinFE, the experiential probability was very high that it would be a winner, which could be at risk by moving the stop up, especially during the first ten days of the trade.

That left a gray area that held only three trades or less than 10% of the small sample. These trades were those that essentially went nowhere, so they were little danger to our capital (see Table 9.1).

TABLE 9.1   CAMPAIGN TRADING PROFITABILITY NEW YORK LIGHT CRUDE, 1984–1994

Mode	Rule	Stop Level	Profit/Loss (points)
Trend	Two moving averages	.31	3,600
Trend	Add-on day-trades	.31	2,500
Trend	Add-on position trades	.31	640
Trend	Reversal	.31	1,827
Range	Trade into range	.31	550
Range	Reverse out of range	.51	2,229
Range	Cut off losing reversal trades	.31	0

---

[5] Without documenting it, I'd say this is my experience. I'm a small fan of moving up stops.

Despite the lack of profit, there were some distinct behavioral characteristics of trades reversing out of ranges. Observations taken along these lines can be done for trending trades and their reversals as well. Who knows? There may be some value to moving up stops when trading those rules.

10
Shifting the Odds: Using Options

A campaigning trader will wish to turn every advantage his or her way, particularly since the costs of trading and the working of time will generally run against the trader. In addition, the market is generally perverse and usually will do whatever it takes to frustrate most of the participants—and one of the most frustrating things is getting your stop picked off by a point or three. Keeping in mind that such a price extreme is likely to be very lightly traded by everyone but you only adds irritation to your losses.

Also, generally, time is not the trader's friend. The longer things go on, the more opportunity there is for things to go wrong. Since only one of three possible outcomes (favorable excursion, no excursion, or adverse excursion) is possible and two of them are bad news,[1] a campaigner will constantly seek tactics that minimize the costs of this fundamental problem. In this chapter, I suggest looking at options.[2]

---

[1] Adverse excursion generates a loss and nonexcursion puts capital at risk for no return, thereby losing the opportunity cost of the capital.

[2] Options traders are due all respect for their particular niche, of which I am not a part! Those wanting expertise in options I refer to Larry McMillan, *Options as a*

RATIONALE FOR USING OPTIONS

The disadvantages to using options spring to mind immediately. They are more thinly traded, their mathematics is intimidating, and their management—given their plethora—can cause real pain and confusion.

One plus is the potential to convert one-third of your possible outcomes to wins rather than losses. That's worth something, but how can it be? Simply put, options' decaying earns money over time. If that time is the period when you have a directional bias, you have the potential to earn some time premium instead of losing the opportunity cost of your money.

Where but in options can you sell something you may not own, that's wasting away, and if you're in futures options, that's a wasting option on a contract with its own time decay? It's a deal, but selling time premium with a view of the underlying's movement is an ongoing, intensively managed process that is beyond the scope of this book. I believe it's really only suitable for full-time professionals, adequately financed, who can constantly roll (that is, close and resell at different strikes and maturities) their positions as the underlying's movements dictate. For such professionals, MAE stops are indicators to terminate their view of the underlying's direction.

The other plus to options is that using an option to stop or reverse a position is more flexible than a clear stop. The material in this book has worked out a process to estimate where stops should go, but I don't pretend that this estimate is precise or that the future will behave precisely as has the past. For example, determining that the stop should be placed precisely 18 ticks from the entry is not precise at all; it is an estimate as vague as the data that generated it. An options's flexibility may help with this situation.

Strategic Investment, 3d ed. (New York: New York Institute of Finance, 1993); Options Laboratory, software developed by Mantic Software, (970) 679-1630; and Options Simulator, software by Bay Options, (510) 845-6425.

I liken the market to the statistician's traditional urn, only this urn is full of multicolored balls. Each day in the market, an event we are monitoring occurs. Perhaps it is the adverse price movement from a given point of entry. As it happens, we have the records of the past, let's say, 1,175 adverse price movements.

Just so, we could have an urn of 1,175 colored balls. Each day a new colored ball could be added to the urn, just as a new price movement is added to our collected history. If we sample the urn's balls, we're going to come up with a distribution of colors, just as we've come up with a distribution of adverse price movements. The troubles are, we don't know what's generating the balls or how the color (the price) is determined. Something uncertain is changing the number and colors of the balls and we don't know how uncertain it is.

Similarly, we don't know what changes the market's prices, for the most part. Plus, we don't know how much the price change will be, if any. This should keep fresh in our minds the vagueness of our estimates of the future.

SETTING UP TO USE OPTIONS

Before diving into options, preparation is important. Particularly if you plan to sell options and hold the positions over time, you're going to manage a fairly complex process of rolling positions for advantage. Frankly, you'll need hardware and software to price and plan your options positions, monitor their current status, and account for their profit and loss. Although good analytical software is available for this, it's not easy to use.[3] Plan on training for a month or so to gain facility.

---

[3] OptionVue IV is probably the best all-around choice for a retail trader's day-to-day use. Option Simulator, either off line or real time, currently has a better interface but no portfolio management capabilities. For learning about options and basic position exploration, try Options Lab. Experienced options traders from institutional settings might go with Optionomics and a separate portfolio management program.

Liquidity

There are also some mechanics to options trading that may not have come up in your trading the underlying instrument, whether it was a stock, an index, or a futures contract. The major problem is lack of liquidity, which means that the pricing you receive may prohibit putting on the position you want, particularly if you are trying to manage an effective stop precisely.

As it happens, Crude oil has a very liquid market in its options, as do Eurodollars, Treasury bonds, D-marks, the OEX, and the S&P 100. Stocks are all over the ballpark, but only the biggest consistently have heavy volume and that around the current price. Ideally, you'd see 10,000 or more a day in the option you'd like to use but, realistically, you're more likely to find 300 to 500.

Although you can use limit orders, the other side of the trade probably isn't interested in giving you a good deal, so be realistic. It may be that using an option for some of the purposes described here just can't be done.

Lack of liquidity away from the heavily traded vehicles also affects stops. Specifically, they are less likely to be executed where you place them, if you use them. While I haven't seen them spuriously picked off in the few markets I trade, their slack execution seems to make it unlikely you'll get the price you expected.

Orders

For many, simply the issuance of options orders, particularly spreads, is confusing. As in all trading, there's no getting around this homework. If you issue a confusing order to your broker, he will try to feed it back to you until it makes sense to him. At that point, it may or may not make sense to *you*, and if you let it slide, what you get may not be what you thought you ordered.

Know what you're doing before you get involved. Practice constructing the positions with your software, as well as preparing and reading out the orders. Some software will actually print the order for you, but you should also be able to place your order verbally, particularly if your broker's parlance is slightly different from the software's.

Monitoring Positions

Because options trade less frequently, there will be a lot less information coming down the data pipe or being displayed in the newspaper. Your option might not even be quoted in the WSJ or IBD. At other times the price shown in the paper may only remotely be close to what, if any, trades went down.

In this situation, your software and your inputs to the software become critical to your knowing where you are. Software that can price your portfolio from the underlying and its volatility will save you a lot of agony. Portfolio software that instead uses a price from two days ago may show a very unrealistic value for your option(s).

You should take any unexpected portfolio values with caution and learn how to check them out on your own. Given that you know where the underlying is, have a good volatility history, and have an accurate interest rate inserted, your software should come up with a good estimate of current value, fairly comparable to the prices reported. If not, suspect your software on your inputs first; market makers rarely get too far from reality.

SKIPPING STOPS, USING OPTIONS

One of the nice things that comes out of seeing your tradable through the lens of your trading rules is that you'll probably find out pretty quickly whether you're correct about the market's direction. Crude oil's losing trades run longer than I've experienced in financials but still are significantly shorter than winning trades, rarely going more than ten days.

In terms of options, that means that the runoff of premium may not be as much a problem as it would be if your options positions were going to last for several months. An option purchased to protect a position until we know whether it's a winner will be in position only for a matter of days, sometimes only one or two days. Time decay is not usually a problem for short-term hedges; much more of the price change comes from changes in the underlying issue.

Calculating Equivalent Positions

Once the MAE stop has been calculated, the straightforward approach is to put it in place and let it work for you. If, in your judgment,[4] you expect a stop to be inadvisable (perhaps because it ends up at a location many other traders are likely to pick, or because the market is experiencing abnormal gaps and daily ranges that could cause gross slippage, or because a sharp breakout is likely),[5] you can sidestep that difficulty by purchasing an option. If your underlying position is long, purchase a put that will make money on the downside and won't be hit by a stop in the underlying market. If short, a call will make money if the trade goes against you and likewise won't be hit by a stop.

Of course, you give up something by buying insurance: the profit you could make on your underlying transaction will be reduced by the loss on your option, your insurance.

As an example, Figure 10.1 shows the traditional options diagrammatic format with a long position and our MAE stop. This diagram shows that as the price of the underlying tradable rises, the value of the long position naturally rises. As it falls, the value declines until the price reaches the point at which an MAE stop has been inserted. The loss taken from the stop's being triggered is shown by the dashed arrow extending to the left toward the vertical axis. The virtue of this tack is simplicity and the cheap nature of stops: without slippage, the cost is simply that of a commission.

---

[4] After all, you didn't include your judgment in your back testing. To start using it now is certainly questionable and alters the size of the losses you're going to take. The central conclusion from the evidence gathered was that winning trades seldom go against you as far as the MAE stop.

[5] As data in Chapter 8 suggested for reversals out of ranges.

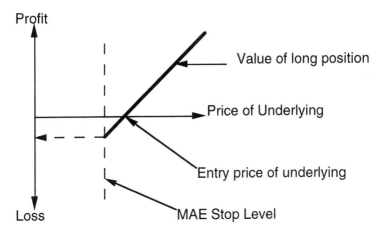

FIGURE 10.1 LONG THE UNDERLYING. Transformed to options format, the position, if it goes bad, it stopped out at the MAE stop level for a loss.

The alternative to a stop for an underlying long is buying a put. Actually, in going long and buying a put, you've just constructed a synthetic option, a call. The long position with the purchased put is equivalent to a simple purchased call. (A short position with a purchased call is equivalent to a simple purchased put.) Yes, it would be simpler to just buy a call if you want to go long (or a put if you want to go short), and there will be fewer lines on the diagram if we use the call only. Figure 10.2 diagrams the options position at expiration, a purchased (i.c., long) call, which is equivalent to a long underlying plus a purchased put.

The diagrams in Figures 10.1 and 10.2 should look very similar to you. Both slant upward as the price of the underlying increases. As the underlying's price decreases, the option's value comes to a minimum because you can't lose more than the cost of the option. The loss on the long position is indicated on the vertical axis to the left.

The difference between the two is that the options position ends in the hole by the amount of the premium in the option. This is shown by the option's value being negative at the point of entry in

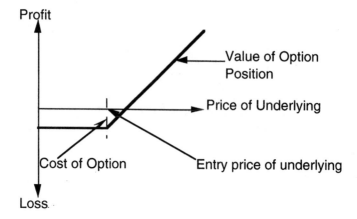

FIGURE 10.2   LONG THE OPTION. Use of an option creates a profit/loss graph of roughly the same shape as an outright position with a stop. The option's cost is the space between the price of the underlying and the lower line of the option's value.

the underlying. As a result, the underlying must advance enough to pay for this cost before you break even. This is the cost of the insurance you've purchased (instead of just using the "free" MAE stop). Figure 10.3 shows the two diagrams together.

If the question is whether to use an option, then when is the option position equivalent to the MAE stop? In Figure 10.4, the MAE stop level is drawn at the price of the underlying that would generate an exit at the same level as the cost of the option at expiration. This is an extreme situation: you buy the option and hold it until expiration, incurring the full cost of the premium. Usually, we wouldn't do this if we knew the underlying trade's risky time horizon was five to ten days as it was in Chapter 9. Usually, the cost of the premium will be less than shown in Figure 10.4.[6]

To elaborate, the cost of using the option grows over time. If you bought the option and sold it tomorrow, without price movement,

---

[6] That is, the horizontal loss line for the option will be higher on the Y axis, closer to zero.

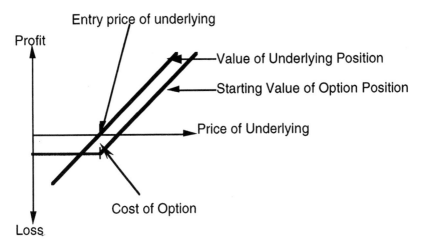

FIGURE 10.3   LESS PROFIT. Although the shapes of the two positions are similar, the two choices' outcomes at the option's expiration are different by the cost of the premium, assuming commissions are roughly similar. The option position's value is less than that of the underlying's if we let it run to expiration—which knowledgeable traders don't need to do.

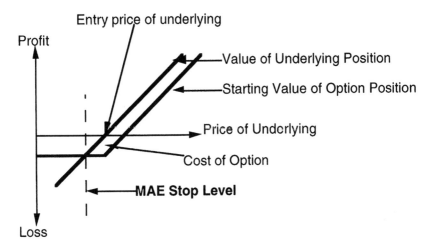

FIGURE 10.4   STOP VS. OPTION. When would the cost of the option be equivalent to the probable cost of the stop? While overly simplified, this diagram depicts the tradeoff between the two.

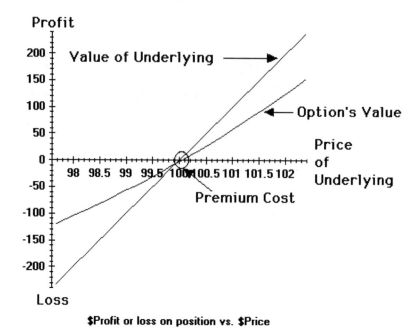

$Profit or loss on position vs. $Price

FIGURE 10.5   VALUES AT OPENING. Without price movement, on the day you open the option position, its liquidation will cost you little premium.

there'd be very little difference in the selling and buying prices (see Figure 10.5). If you sold the option after one-third of its remaining life, without underlying price movement, there'd be a bigger difference (see Figure 10.6). If you sold it close to expiration, there'd be quite a big difference (see Figure 10.7).

This is good news. When looking at a stop versus an option, keep in mind that our horizon for insurance coverage is 10 to 20 days and our price range 30 to 40 ticks. The premium decay is likely to be small.[7] If so, the cost of using the option (in this example, buying a call) isn't going to be the full premium. Our knowl-

---

[7] Unless we've used an option expiring in the next 20 or 30 days.

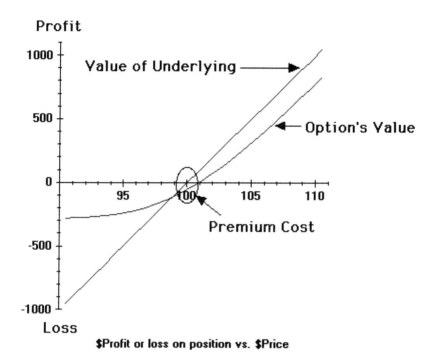

$Profit or loss on position vs. $Price

FIGURE 10.6   AFTER ONE-THIRD OF OPTION'S LIFE. (18 days.) If you liquidate the option now, you will get back less as the gap between the original price and the current price widens. After 18 days, the cost of the option is still small.

edge of the amount of the loss to be covered and the time frame in which we're trading opens an opportunity for us.

That said, we still need to make the comparison between the known amount of the stop (times its probability of exercise) and the probable cost of the option if it's exercised. Your options software can deal with your specific situation in depth. Here, we'll explore the alternatives generically.

Before getting into that, however, let's consider commissions. The costs of buying a call instead of going long the underlying and purchasing a put are compared in Table 10.1, demonstrating that it's slightly cheaper to just do the option.

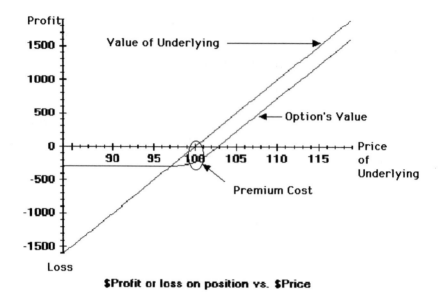

$Profit or loss on position vs. $Price

FIGURE 10.7   ALMOST AT EXPIRATION. (54 days.) Just 2 days before expiration, liquidating the option with the underlying still at 100 would cost almost the entire premium.

Losers

Now let's see how this works in practice. Figure 10.2 is a comparison of outcomes for losing trades, the ones likely to hit the MAE stop. One case would be where the trade hits the MAE stop and goes on to become, as we expect, a loser. The other case we're

TABLE 10.1   COST FACTORS WHEN COVERING TRADES

	Outright with MAE Stop	Outright Covered by Option Hedge	Option Equivalent
Commissions	Entry and stop execution	Entry and option purchase	Option purchase
Premium decay	None	Negligible	Negligible

TABLE 10.2   ROUGH COMPARISON OF COVERING COSTS

Case	Outright Long with MAE Stop	Outright Long Covered by Put Costing .38	Option Equivalent: a Purchased Call at .38
Underlying falls to MAE stop level .30 but not to .40. *Recovers to win.*	Position sold at MAE stop for loss of .3.	Profit on underlying reduced by loss on option (up to .38).[9]	Profit on position up to .38 less than outright.[10]
Underlying falls to MAE stop level .30 and falls to .40 below entry before we close out *at a loss.*	Position sold at MAE stop for a loss of .30	Loss of .40 on the underlying less a gain of .19 on the put[11] = net loss of .21.	Loss of .5 × = .19 on the call.

greedily trying to save is the one where it hits the stop but goes on to become a winner. Table 10.2 shows tabular outcomes for each case, excluding commissions, assuming we want to be long with an MAE stop of .30.[8]

Seen this way, options take the steam out of a fall to the downside, at least when used in a 1:1 ratio with the underlying. If you wanted

---

[8] For the options-enabled reader. I'm assuming an at-the-money purchase of either the put or call.

[9] Most likely the cost would be much less. The trade probably won't last until expiration, and many would sell the option when the trade took on winning characteristics such as the MinFE exceeding .3 for reversal trades.

[10] Actually .38 less than the outright had it not been stopped out.

[11] Assuming a delta of .5, the rough estimate would be .19 = .38 × .5. This would only be precisely correct if the underlying were right at the strike price when bought. Traders who wanted closer-to-dollar-for-dollar coverage (i.e., delta closer to 1) would use an in-the-money put.

Using an away-from-the-money put is a neat way to get a delta that will get the

roughly the same price movement from the options as the underlying, you'd adjust the number of options and/or the strike price.

More sophisticated approaches than using an at-the-money option are possible.[12] For the short-term speculative trader worried about the 3 to 5 days after entry, however, it may be enough to look at the known cost of the insurance (maximum .38 on the downside, probably much less), the loss level the trader is trying to manage to (e.g., .30), and the hoped-for short-term gain in the next 10 to 20 trading days (e.g., 1.20). If the underlying moves against the trader, the loss is likely to be .19 or at worst .38 if he or she just keeps holding the option, looking for a more opportune exit. This is cheap.

That the net cost of using the option in a losing situation might not be the entire premium, and that the cost might even be less than the stop is good news on the downside, but what happens on the upside?

Winners

Things are more complicated on the upside. If the trade moves his or her way and the trader is long the call; he or she must return to the complexity mentioned above: the option will not move upward as fast as the underlying would. Initially, it might move only half as fast. As the trade advanced and the option got deeper into the money, it might start moving 70%, 80%, or 90% as fast as the underlying. If the trader were to hold it deeply into the money until expiration, the net profit on buying the call would approximate the

---

trading cost of the option into the range of the amount we want to spend on loss control. If the ATM option has delta of .5, we'll be down 50% when the underlying hits our stop level. If that's too expensive, an OOTM option might have a delta of .3. If 50% is really cheap compared to MAE stop, an ITM option might have a delta of .8.

[12] Using a deep in- or out-of-the-money option with its different delta to match the exposure you like would be one example. A ratio of long and short options might cover a specific price range. Knowing the area of price excursion from entry that must be protected gives the options trader some specificity in constructing an options position.

value of the underlying long less the cost of the option. Because winning reversals out of ranges (as an example) run from 15 to 65 days, this would be common.

In the near term, the "long the underlying, purchase a put" strategy has one advantage over the "purchase a call" strategy: on the near-term upside, it participates 1:1 with the rise of the underlying (less the cost of the insuring put) while the purchased call equivalent will have a .5:1 participation, roughly speaking, with the rise of the underlying.

One effect works to the trader's advantage: the sooner the trader can unload the position (when the trading signal for the underlying flashes *exit* by hitting the stop), the more premium he or she can recover selling the option. Another effect works against the trader: the further into the money the option goes (and the more time that necessarily takes), the less premium he or she can recover selling the option. The short time frame of the Crude reversal trade works for the trader; success—involving more time—works against the option position. Net of both effects, the trader will undoubtedly recover some premium in selling the position, reducing the cost of his original insurance. Table 10.3 shows an example (without commissions) if the trader went long at 17.00.

On the upside, the outright is always ahead of the purchased call strategy by some portion of the premium. Eventually, the pre-

TABLE 10.3   COMPARING AN OUTRIGHT TO AN OPTION

Price of Crude	Days into Trade	Value of Long Crude at 17.00	Value of Long Call Bought at .38	Profit of Long Call Bought at .38	Advantage of Underlying Long vs. Long Call
17.00	0	0	.38	0	0 – 0 = 0
17.50	5	.50	.74[13]	.74 – .38 = .36	.50 – .36 = .14
18.00	10	1.00	1.12	1.12 – .38 = .74	1 – .74 = .26
18.50	15	1.50	1.58	1.58 – .38 = 1.20	1.5 – 1.20 = .30
19.00	20	2.00	2.04	2.04 – .38 = 1.66	2 – 1.66 = .34

---

[13] .74 = .50 intrinsic value (17.50 – 17.00) + .24 premium. These values are exemplary.

mium would wear away until the outright's advantage over the option would be .38, the original cost. The purchased call cushions you on the downside and, on the upside, incurs a greater premium cost as the trade wears on while participating in the gain more slowly than the underlying.

Had you bought Crude and purchased a put for protection then seen Crude advance like this, you'd have, without commissions, something close to the values shown in Table 10.4. In other words, you suffer the erosion of the premium in a way very similar to that of just holding the call, reinforcing the equivalence of a purchased call with the "buy Crude and buy a put" approach.

If your knowledge of Crude's behavior indicates that a trade is likely to be a winner, you could take off the put protection earlier or convert the call. For example, range-reversal trades lasting ten days are rarely losers. Reversals with a MinFE greater than .1 are sometimes but rarely losers. These are chances to increase profit by dropping your insurance coverage even though you were covered during the hazardous five or ten days after entry.

Bottom Line

The second-to-the-bottom line is that the cost to the trader of short-term usage of the option in a favorable trade is likely to be

TABLE 10.4   COMPARING AN OUTRIGHT TO OUTRIGHT PLUS OPTION

Price of Crude	Days into Trade	Value of Long Crude at 17.00	Value of Long Put Bought at .38	Profit of Long Put Bought at .38	Advantage of Underlying Long vs. Long Underlying and Long Put
17.00	0	0	.38	0	0
17.50	5	.50	.23	.23−.38 = −.15	.5− (.5 − .15) = −.15
18.00	10	1.00	.1	.1 − .38 = −.28	1 − (1 − .28) = −.28
18.50	15	1.50	.04	.04 − .38 = −.34	1.5− (1.5 − .34) = −.34
19.00	20	2.00	.01	.01 − .38 = −.37	2 − (2 − .37) = −.37

low—certainly not the entire premium—if the trade is a loser. A Crude trader who knows that the time horizon to use the option is five to ten days has a tremendous advantage: if the trade fails, the cost of protection is likely to be less than the MAE stop (but never more than the cost of the option), but if the trade is a winner, he or she doesn't necessarily pay the entire cost of the premium (and never more than the premium).

The bottom line is that an option will cost the trader something but it may be comparable to the cost of a stop. Comparing the option to a two in three chance (or whatever your loss/win ratio is) of hitting the stop is, in the case of a Crude reversal trade, just about a draw:

2/3 chance of MAE hit at .31 @ .20

versus

{an expected option loss of .19 (on a loser)
and a .3 lesser profit (on a winner)}

which works out to:

.20

versus

{2/3 * .19 + 1/3 * .3 = .22}

These numbers are too rough to take as other than an indicator for judgment. The trader who doesn't want the stop picked or is in a very confused market can use an option instead without fearing exorbitant cost. In the 11-year test period, the limited evidence suggests he or she would be just as well off using an option as when using a stop and, in a fast market, might be better off.

Each market will differ, and because volatility of the markets changes, the pricing of the options changes, which affects the comparison with the use of a stop. If the option is very expensive, use the stop. If volatility is low and the option is cheap, use the option.

The Evidence

What we learned in earlier chapters about how Crude behaves when we trade a certain way is useful. Because we know the duration of our trades, we know options are likely to cost less than they seem to cost and may be competitive with stops. Because we know the trading rules' success rate, we can estimate whether options are more likely to be useful than stops. Most important, because we know where our stop/reversal point is, we can objectively compare options versus outrights.

TRADING

The examples in this chapter show an approach to using options on Crude reversal trades. The conclusion might be completely different for a different tradable, a different interest-rate environment, a different implied volatility in Crude, or a different MAE stop. Although much can be automated to speed up analysis, there is no general rule. Options fade in and out of your tactical tool bag, requiring your art and judgment in employing them. As it happens, in Crude range-reversal trades, you have the flexibility to use either the stop or the option, the only difference being that in using the option you will certainly pay for the insurance, whereas with the stop you may avoid paying any insurance.

Options do increase the analytical workload on the campaigner, particularly if more exotic combinations than described here are used. Traders not set up to handle this complexity might find it justifiable to skip options on that basis alone.

Regarding the profit impact of using options on Crude reversal trades, there are no additional profits from using them. In campaigning with Crude, they might be viable on, say, trend trades or add-on trades or trend reversals, but not on range-reversal trades.

This chapter has shown only the idea of using options and has given an example of testing them on one of the tactics of campaign trading: reversals out of range. An active campaigner will check out whether options should be used for every tactic he or she employs.

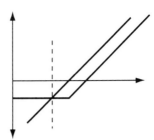

11
Conclusion to Campaign Trading

Whether in a trending mode or a ranging mode, the Crude market behaves characteristically when viewed through the simple trading rules used here. As an example of campaigning, Crude showed many of the behaviors a veteran campaigner would exploit.

It turned out you could trade Crude as a trending market, but you could also add additional trades to the trending mode either from the short-term average or the long-term average. You could also reverse out of trending trades profitably.

When the market shifted to ranging mode, there was a much smaller set of trades into the range, but there weren't enough trades to add on to range trades. You could reverse out of the range, though, and that turned out to be a very profitable exercise.

Examining minimum favorable excursion clearly identified winning trades when reversing out of range, but there were too few cases in that mode where this technique proved useful. Applied to other modes such as add-on trades from the short-term average, MinFE might be of more use. Although no general rules were shown, graphs of price excursion for winning and losing trades both showed characteristic behaviors, running in channels that could be informative to a trader using judgment in managing trades.

Crude also has a strong options market that gives the campaigner some flexibility in managing a position, though in the single example in Chapter 10, the trader could have used either options or stops equivalently. Each situation would need to be examined independently in the future.

SEEING THE MARKET

Leaving aside Crude as a campaign vehicle, the most important lesson is to transform market behavior so that it's measured from the point of entry of an explicit set of rules. Only then can you see the market in your terms.

Next, measure and chart the price excursion from that point of entry to see if there is a distinct difference between the behavior of winning trades and losing trades. As Crude showed, you'd like the worst adverse excursion of winning trades to be sharply different from that of losing trades. Similarly, you'd like the least favorable excursion of winning trades to be sharply different from that of losing trades. This is information you can use.

You use it in the case of adverse excursion by identifying losers quickly with an experience-based stop that cuts losers before they do great damage but without unnecessarily cutting off winners. In the case of favorable excursion, you identify winners early on so you can move up stops and minimize losses without cutting off winners.

CAMPAIGN TACTICS

Every possible campaign tactic hasn't been covered. Option writing to exploit the directional information stops give you was too complicated to include. Betting strategies[1] weren't either; only add-on trades had nearly enough trades to attempt this. Countertrading into the trend was left to the reader.

---

[1] Principally, martingales, a sequence of varying bet sizes designed to end profitably.

Still, the basics are all present in New York Light Crude: trend and ranging, add-ons and reverses. A trader who doesn't want to be restricted to just one strategy can have two here: trending or ranging. A trader who wants a variety of tactics to exploit can have three: the fundamental trade (trend or into the range), the add-on trade, and the reversal trade.

The result should be an active campaigner steadily building strength with limited losses.

Even with just one trading vehicle, it's possible to have several trades going at once, and add-on trades alone could keep the trader glued to the trading desk. Include several tradables—or hundreds—and there is ample opportunity for diversification of trading tactics, as well as diversification of trading vehicles.

OLD HANDS

The tactics tested in this book are common among experienced traders, who learned them from experience. The price excursion technique simply puts a picture to the price behavior and gives usable information to execute old trading maxims, with some rational approach.

I realize this material does not provide one simple rule for all situations—the retail trader's dream. Constructing and analyzing distributions is a lot of work; it's as messy as reality. Still, I hope others will expand this introduction and develop more useful ways to capture the behavior of their trading market and use it for profit.

This approach is the only consistent framework I know within which a campaign of trading—trading in all market modes—can be undertaken. Whatever the market's mode, whatever the tactic you employ, excursion analysis shows you where to get the edge on the market so you can win with minimal losses. Only with this capability can you trade more or less continuously, constantly building strength rather than waiting for congenial market conditions.

Within this framework, diversification of trading vehicles makes practical sense, and not just from some hopeful lack of correlation. In this framework, with all vehicles working most of the time, not only may losses on one vehicle offset gains on another, but more likely, steady gains in all vehicles will amplify each other.

A campaign turns a trading vehicle from a sporadic contributor to your strength to something more reliable.

Indeed, without analyzing price excursion from entry, the whole notion of campaigning as I've described it is not viable. Excursion analysis unites all the disparate tactics and strategy, all the brief trades with the long engagements, in a simple nuts-and-bolts method to control losses so that the action of the market can take our bank accounts where we want them to go.

Appendix:
Trading Charts

To prepare data for this analysis and the resultant trading, I first determined (see Chapter 4) that the two months prior to expiration were the months to follow when trading the New York Light Crude contracts (That is, we trade the June contract in April). Then I assembled sequences of those months for all 11 contract years. On the last day of the month, I used the spread between the expiring[1] contract (e.g., September) and the contract to be picked up (e.g., October) to adjust the new contract's values so that the change between the days (September 30 and October 1) was the same as in the expiring contract. Figures A.1–A.13 also show the 12-day and 58-day simple moving averages used in the exemplary trading.

In actually trading this information, you work backward, adjusting the old data to synchronize with the current contract. This allows you to trade off today's quotes with no adjustments.

The resulting continuous contracts look different from the actual historical contracts, and I include them here so that the reader can make a quick visual search for anything he or she would consider anomalous.

---

[1] The contract doesn't expire until the month before the nominal month. For example, the November contract stops trading in October, and for analysis and actual trading, we'd trade the November contract in September.

Data for this work were generously supplied on a very timely basis by both CSI and Dial Data, to whom I give many thanks. Anomalies you may find, if any, are most likely the result of my machinations rather than data errors.

The data were extracted from the vendors' download files, manipulated in Microsoft Excel for the Macintosh into continuous data series, transferred to DOS ASCII files and uploaded into MetaStock for Windows[2] using Equis's downloader utility. Although I have mistakenly been quoted as favoring these vendors above all others, in fact, many other vendors could have handled these tasks, and my choices here were ones of convenience and familiarity rather than capability.

There's usually someone who would like the actual numbers. They are available until April 1999. Contact me at Nail56@AOL.COM.

---

[2] MetaStock for Windows, of which I used a very early version, had a minor bug in that the price scale needed to be reset manually to show the correct values. I believe I caught all those instances, but if not, that may explain values extremely at variance to the reader's experience.

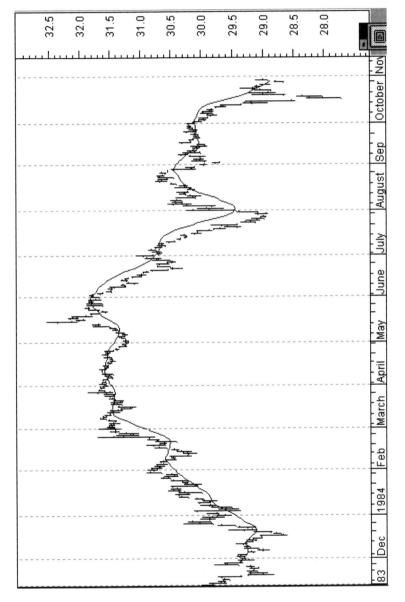

FIGURE A.1 1984.

230

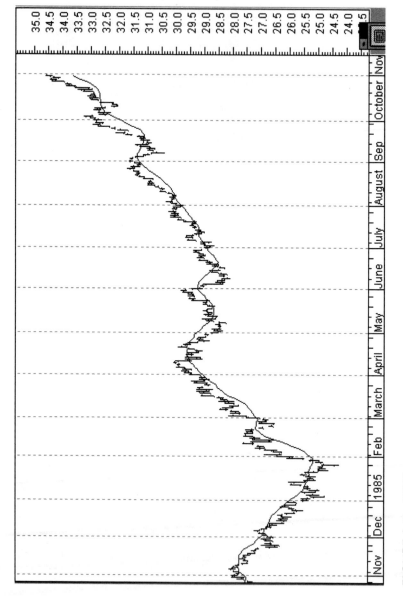

FIGURE A.2   1985.

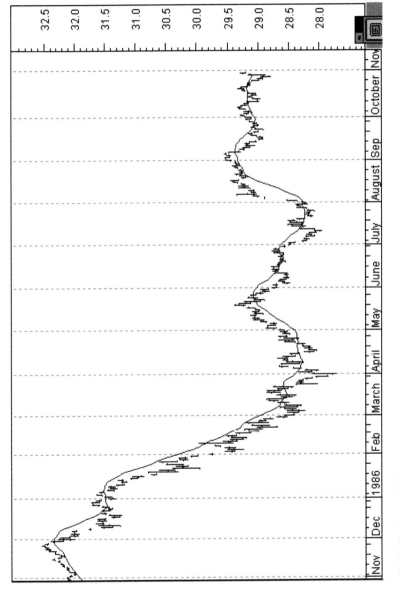

FIGURE A.3   1986.

232

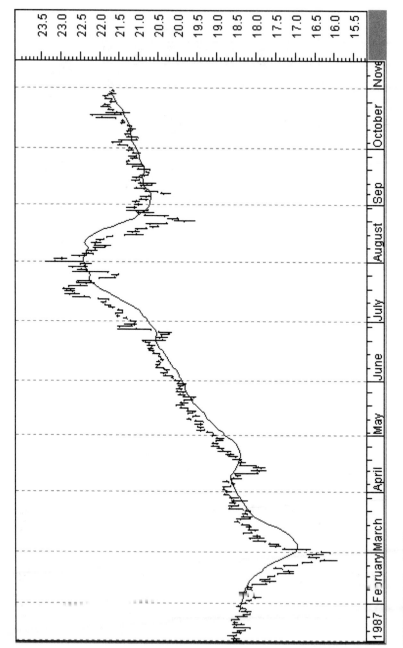

FIGURE A.4 1987.

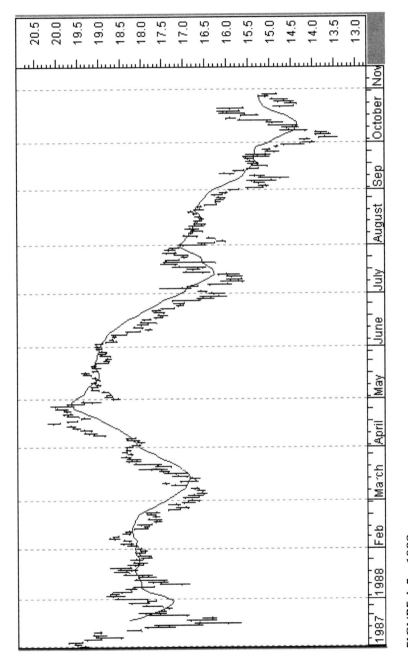

FIGURE A.5 1988.

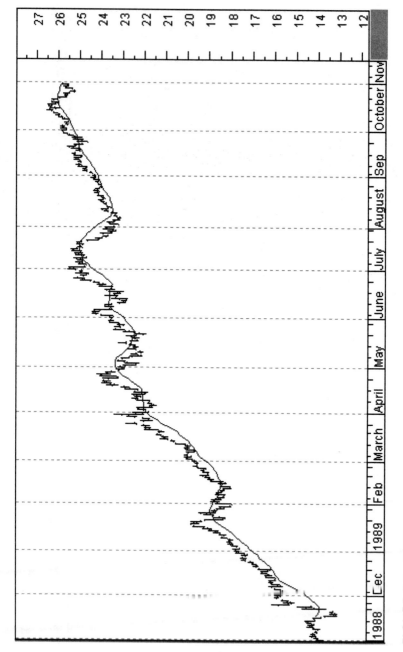

FIGURE A.6 1989.

234

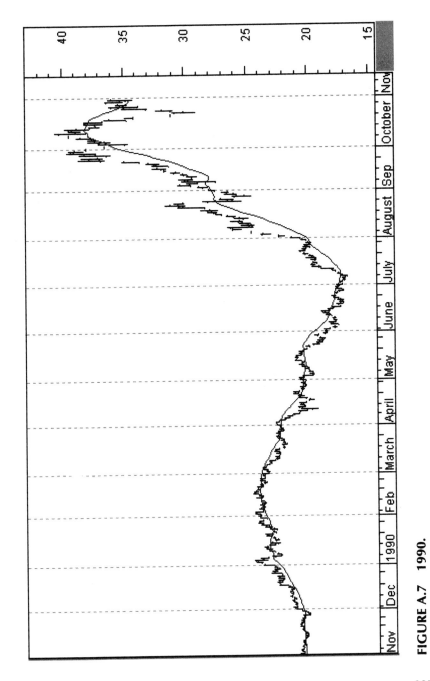

FIGURE A.7 1990.

235

236

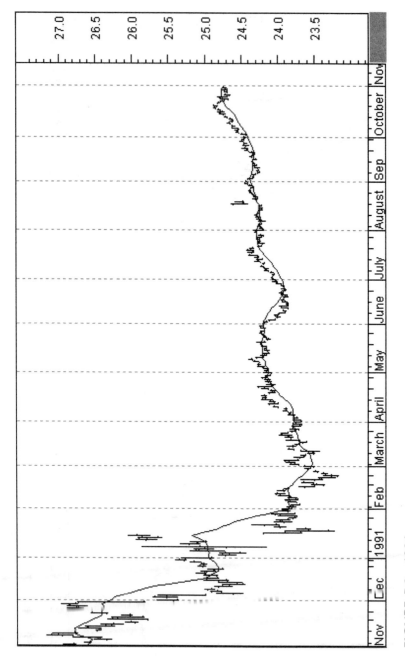

FIGURE A.8 1991.

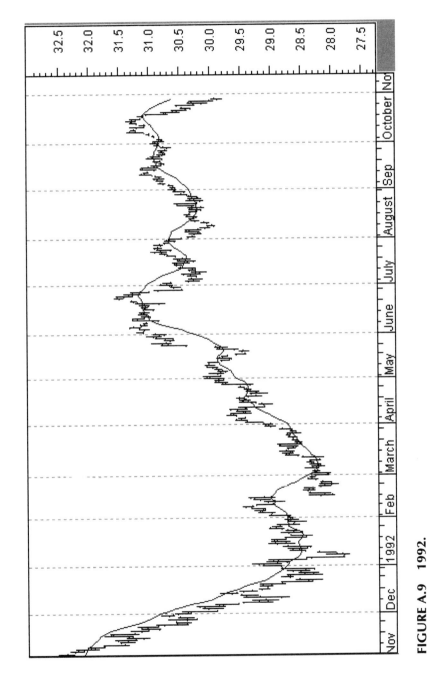

FIGURE A.9   1992.

237

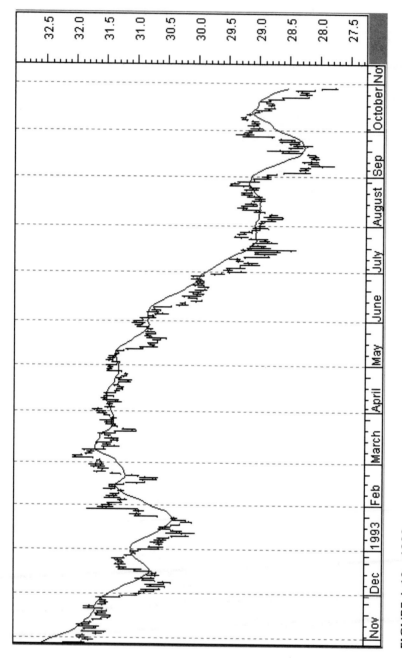

FIGURE A.10 1993.

238

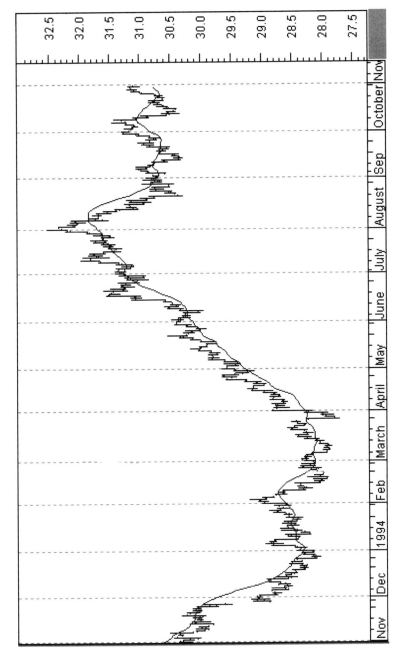

FIGURE A.11   1994.

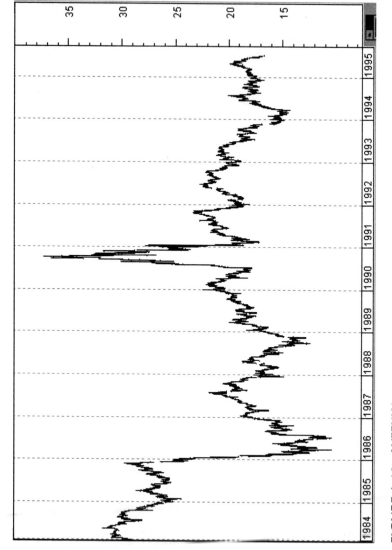

FIGURE A.12   WEEKLY.

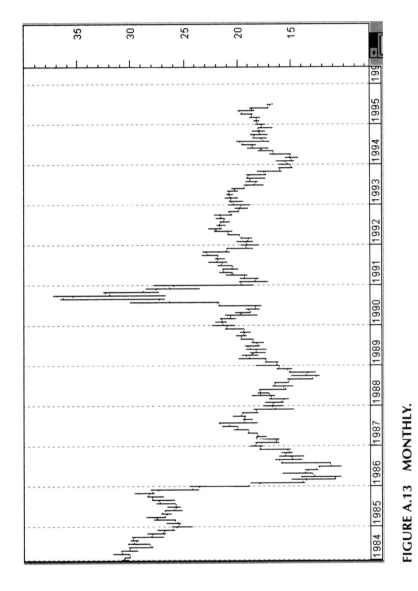

FIGURE A.13 MONTHLY.

Index